Flowers that Wow

Flowers that Wow

Inspired Arrangements for the Floral-Impaired

Jonathan Fong

Photography by Jessica Boone

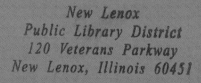
Watson-Guptill Publications / New York

Senior acquisitions editor: Joy Aquilino
Edited by Patricia Fogarty
Designed by Pooja Bakri/Bakri Design
Graphic production by Joseph Illidge
Photography by Jessica Boone

First published in 2006 by
Watson-Guptill Publications,
a division of VNU Business Media, Inc.,
770 Broadway, New York, NY 10003
www.watsonguptill.com

Library of Congress Cataloging-in-Publication Data

Fong, Jonathan.
  Flowers that wow : inspired arrangements for the
  floral-impaired / By Jonathan Fong.
     p. cm.
  ISBN-13: 978-0-8230-6985-9
  ISBN-10: 0-8230-6985-0
  1. Flower arrangement. I. Title.
  SB449.F57 2006
  745.92—dc22

                              2006010186

Printed in Malaysia   **3 1984 00247 1546**

First printing, 2006

1 2 3 4 5 6 7 8 9 / 14 13 12 11 10 09 08 07 06

contents

Introduction

Until five years ago, I had never made a floral arrangement. It had never even occurred to me. I certainly loved flowers, but I bought them at the florist, not imagining that I could create an arrangement myself. I wouldn't have even known where to start.

At the time, I was working in an advertising agency that employed a few hundred people, so it was inevitable that practically every day, at the reception desk, there would be a delivery of flowers for someone from a significant other or a sales rep. My co-workers often stopped to admire the flowers and peek at the cards to see who they were from. Inquisitive me, I began poking my finger inside the arrangements to see how they were made. What I learned was that on the outside they may have been gorgeous, but on the inside, they were supported by a very unglamorous infrastructure of floral foam, tape, and pins. It seemed as long as there was floral foam, you could do anything. I thought, "How hard can this be? And I'll bet I can do it for a lot cheaper than they're charging."

So I took the plunge. I was having an Easter dinner for friends, and I figured it would be the perfect opportunity to try out my "have floral foam, can do anything" theory. I stocked up on floral foam from the crafts store and then headed downtown to the Los Angeles Flower Mart during public hours, buying as many flowers as my scrawny arms could hold. It was time to experiment.

That weekend, I became a floral designer. My friends couldn't believe what I had created. Heck, *I* couldn't believe it. Stripped of their mystery, floral arrangements were a lot easier, and cheaper, than I had imagined.

Emboldened by my first success, I tried other floral projects. Sure, I concocted a few hideous eyesores along the way, but for the most part I was having a blast. And as I shared my creations on my website, www.jonathanfongstyle.com, I received such an enthusiastic response from flower lovers around the world that I knew I was not alone in wanting to craft fun and fabulous florals.

This book demonstrates some very untraditional uses of flowers that expand the definition of what a floral arrangement is—from a Bollywood-inspired curtain of marigolds, to a turkey centerpiece, to a floral gown. I use both fresh and artificial flowers, depending on the project. Although I specify what flowers to use, most projects are pretty adaptable, allowing you to substitute the flowers that are in season and available in your area.

And you will love how easy the projects are. My step-by-step instructions may not be how the pros do it, but these simple guidelines worked for a novice like me, so I know they'll work for you.

I've indicated the approximate time it will take to complete each project, as well as the "level of ease," ranging from 1 to 5, with 1 being the easiest. There's no "level of difficulty" here.

1 **IT DOESN'T GET ANY EASIER THAN THIS.**

2 **EASY AS PIE.**

3 **SO EASY, YOU'LL FEEL LIKE YOU DESERVE YOUR OWN TV SHOW.**

4 **A LOT EASIER THAN YOU THOUGHT IT WOULD BE.**

5 **EASY—IF YOU FOLLOW MY DIRECTIONS.**

I've even recommended a snack you can munch on while you tackle each project. Nothing inspires creativity like carbs.

I've also included contributions from some of my favorite floral designers, so they can share their expertise. While I was writing this book, they told me a lot of their trade secrets and swore me to secrecy, so of course I've revealed them to you.

Because I've learned from my mistakes, I've added to some of the chapters a feature called Broadway's Bloopers, named after my trusty canine companion. Here, I share flubs commonly made while creating the arrangements, and how to fix them. Broadway does want me to clarify that although she has kindly lent her name to this section, she is not personally responsible for the bloopers shown.

All in all, I hope you'll be inspired to try these projects yourself or, better yet, to put your own spin on them. We don't have to sit around waiting for someone to send us flowers anymore. We can make our own creations. And that, my friends, is what makes these arrangements truly flowers that wow.

The Shopping List:
Essential Tools and Supplies

I don't believe in advising you to go out and buy a bunch of expensive supplies that you'll use only once or twice. So here are just a few essentials you'll need to start creating the arrangements in this book. Individual projects may require additional elements, but these are the basic supplies I use all the time.

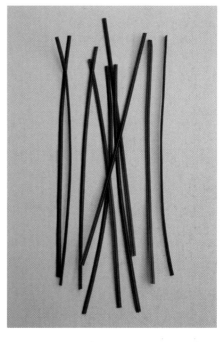

Floral Foam

Repeat after me: "Floral foam is my friend." It's a miracle product. There are two main brands of floral foam—Oasis and Aqua Foam. I use either one. There are also two types: wet foam (pictured above in the photo), which is soaked in water and used for fresh flowers, and dry foam (pictured below in the photo), which is used for artificial flowers. In this book, whenever the instructions call for floral foam, I mean the wet stuff. When the project involves artificial flowers, I will specifically list "dry" floral foam.

Both types come in standard-sized rectangular bricks. Wet foam is 4¼ inches wide, 9 inches long, and 3 inches high. Dry foam is slightly smaller at 3⅞ inches wide, 7⅞ inches long, and 2¾ inches high. These are the only sizes the bricks come in. While floral supply and crafts stores typically carry dry foam in other shapes, like balls and cones, it is more difficult to find wet foam in other shapes. That's why for the projects in this book that require spheres (like the topiary in chapter 11), I simply carve the rectangular brick into a ball shape.

Greening Pins

These pins hold down moss and ivy in your arrangements. Just place the foliage on the floral foam and secure it by sticking the pin into the foam. Actually, you can use any wire and bend it into a U shape, and that'll do the trick.

Twist Ties

I use twist ties all the time because they're so easy to use for tying floral stems together. Besides, they're great to have on hand for a variety of household uses.

Floral Shears

Invest in a good pair of floral shears. Their sturdy blades are made for cutting through thick stems. Before I had a pair, I ruined some perfectly good sewing scissors thinking they'd do the job. Some florists prefer using a sharp knife to cut stems, but I'm a bit of a klutz when it comes to sharp objects, so I prefer shears.

Buying Flowers

While creating the projects for this book, I purposely chose very common, everyday flowers that are available everywhere. Roses, carnations, mums, and pom-poms may not be the most exotic flowers, but you will be able to find them easily in your local stores. You don't need fancy flowers to create fancy arrangements. In the few cases where I call for more specialized flowers, don't worry. I also suggest other varieties that will create a similar effect.

Where should you buy flowers? When I need to buy in bulk, I buy mine primarily at the Los Angeles Flower Mart. If you have a wholesale flower district in your city, check the hours that the market is open to the general public. (You can usually find the information online.) In my town, the stalls open to the trade starting at 2:00 A.M., and then open to the public later, around 8:00 A.M.

Unless you're creating multiple arrangements for big events, chances are you will never need to buy in bulk. But if you do, and you're not near a wholesale flower district, talk to the growers who sell flowers at your neighborhood farmers' market. I once had to buy 600 potted herbs for herb garden centerpieces, and the vendor at the farmers' market was only too happy to oblige. She even delivered!

For most projects, I find that supermarkets, farmers' markets, and warehouse stores like Costco usually have a great selection. In fact, my local Trader Joe's often sells flowers for less than I can get them at the flower mart. There are also often good deals on a variety of cut flowers at home improvement warehouses like Home Depot. It's a big change from the old days, when you could buy flowers only from a florist.

Stem Wire

Stem wire helps Gerber daisies and other flowers with long stems stay upright. Just insert the end of the wire at the base of the flower and wrap the wire around the length of the stem. You can also cut the wire into smaller pieces and bend them to make your own greening pins.

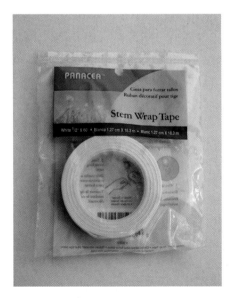

Stem Wrap Tape

This tape is perfect for wrapping stems to each other to create a bouquet. I frequently make bouquets without this tape, but when I want a tightly packed arrangement, the tape holds all the stems together securely. You simply wrap the tape around one stem, add a second stem so the tape is around two stems, and so on until the tape is around the entire bouquet. The tape has very low adhesion so it's easy to work with.

Floral Tape

Tape is helpful when securing floral foam to a base (as with the topiary in chapter 11). It's waterproof, so it stays in place. There is also clear floral tape, which is great for using on glass vases because it's practically invisible.

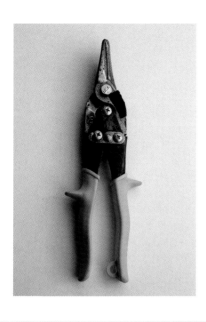

Metal Snips

If you've ever tried to cut the stems of silk flowers, you know how difficult it can be. Because the stems are made of wire, you need wire cutters or metal snips, which is what I use. Protect your eyes when cutting. The stems can fly around wildly when they snap off.

On Sticking Flowers into Floral Foam

In the projects on the following pages, there are basically two ways to insert flowers into the foam—what I call the Straight-in Method and the Angled Method.

Straight-in Method

With this method, you insert the stems perpendicular to the floral foam. This gives you a straight, flat plane of densely packed flowers that form what's known as a "pave" arrangement. The floral baby blocks in chapter 4 and the Warhol arrangement in chapter 5 follow this pave style. The Straight-in Method also results in the flat sides of the floral cake in chapter 1.

Angled Method

As you can see from the photo, the Angled Method allows you to create a rounded shape, even when the floral foam is flat. Here, the stems are placed at gradual angles, with the bottom stems angled horizontally and the top stems angled vertically. This dome shape is ideal for most arrangements because the profile is so full, and the angled flowers hide the stems that are underneath. You can also use the Angled Method in vase arrangements with water. The flowers on the side are angled more, while the taller ones in the middle stand more vertically.

Part One

Flowers for All Occasions

During the year, there is a holiday practically every day, from the nationally recognized to the obscure. Add in celebrations like birthdays and anniversaries, and you've got a very busy social calendar.

We love occasions because they not only commemorate something special, they give us a chance to see friends, perhaps dress up, and in some cases even get a day or two off work. And now they're an excuse to flex your creativity with some unique floral arrangements.

Chapter 1

Snappy Birthdays

Your birthday is the best day in the world. For one magical twenty-four-hour period, it's all about you. People wish you well, friends take you to lunch or dinner, cards arrive in the mail, and you get to open presents.

Birthdays are such a big deal for me probably because I never had a birthday party growing up. Not as a child, cute as I was. Not during high school. Not even in college, or the years after. It wasn't until my thirty-sixth birthday that friends threw me a surprise party. (I know you're trying to decide what's more unbelievable, the fact that I never had a birthday party or that I'm a day over twenty-nine.) So you can see why birthdays are so important to me now. I'm making up for lost time.

Floral Cake

WHAT YOU'LL NEED

45 carnations (approx.): 30 of one color,
  15 of another
8 pom-poms
A bunch of flat flowers—for example, mums,
  daisies, and/or spray roses
½ brick of floral foam
Cake platter

Here's a cake made not with flour, but with flowers. The floral cake is one of my absolute favorite projects. And people love receiving it. (But you have to remind them it's not edible.) It's the perfect gift for that person who has everything. Displayed on a cake pedestal, it also makes a glorious centerpiece for a party. And as impressive as it looks, making one yourself is, well, a piece of cake.

1 The foundation of the cake is our friend, floral foam. First, carve the floral foam into a cake-shaped cylinder so you can put flowers around it. A standard brick is about 4 inches wide, which happens to be the perfect diameter for the cylinder. You may think that the 4-inch cylinder is really small, but keep in mind that when you stick flowers in it, they will extend the diameter of the cake about 2 inches on the sides and on top. Find a can or canister lid that's as wide as the floral foam and, using it as a guide, trace a circle on top of the foam. Then, using a knife (I use a steak knife), shave the sides until you've created a cylinder. Next, soak the foam in water, and place it on a cake platter.

Helpful Hint

When soaking floral foam, place it in a sink full of water and let it absorb the water naturally. It takes only seconds, but the longer you leave it in water the better. Don't force the foam under the water, or you'll create pockets of air in the foam and reduce the amount of water the foam will hold.

2   Carnations are ideal for the sides of the cake because they're inexpensive, they last a long time, and, best of all, they look like frosting. I like to use one color for the top two rows, and another color for the bottom. That way, it looks like there's a frosting trim at the bottom, just like real cakes have.

     Let's start with the bottom row. Cut the carnations, leaving about an inch of the stem, and insert the stem into the foam, pushing the flower in until it can't go any farther. Be sure to use the Straight-in Method explained on page 13, so the sides of your cake will be straight up and down.

3   After completing the bottom row, move to the next row up, using the other color of carnations. Just continue on top of the first layer and insert the flowers so they line up.

4   When the second layer of carnations is in place, insert a third row of carnations on top of the second to complete the sides of the cake.

5   Now let's decorate the cake. Insert a small pom-pom into the floral foam, tucking it in between the first and second layer of carnations. Then every few inches, add another pom-pom until you've encircled the cake with these "polka dots."

❧ *Florist Secret*

When assembling a floral arrangement like the floral cake (or any vase arrangement, for that matter), place it on a lazy susan so you can easily rotate the entire piece as you work. Your arrangement will be more balanced (and it's so much fun to spin it).

6 You can see that your cake is already taking shape, but it's the flowers on top that make it a masterpiece. I used to favor red roses because they looked like strawberries. But now I prefer flatter flowers like daisies and mums because the flatter top is more cake-like. And if I do use roses, they're the smaller spray roses, which provide a flatter silhouette.

Start by inserting flowers at the outer circumference and work inward, to make sure you create a nice frame for the top. Then add flowers until you've filled the empty space.

7 Because some carnations are naturally larger than others, parts of the cake may bulge slightly. No problem. Just take a pair of scissors and trim the cake as though you're trimming a hedge. The carnation shavings will fall and look like coconut shavings. Leave them around the circumference of the cake platter, and they'll add to the festive look.

ANOTHER IDEA

You can also put your floral cake on a plastic plate and place the entire creation in a pastry box (pink is nice if you can get it). It's a great way to present the cake as a hostess gift. The playful packaging also helps keep the cake secure in case you have to travel.

Broadway's Bloopers

The most common mistake in making the floral cake is not inserting the carnations straight in. If the flowers are placed at an angle, the cake becomes more of a dome, as in the photo here.

Rose Petal Balloons

LEVEL OF EASE: 1
ETW (ESTIMATED TIME OF WOW): 5 minutes
RECOMMENDED SNACK: Chex Party Mix

WHAT YOU'LL NEED

6–8 rose petals per balloon
Helium balloons
Super 77 Spray Adhesive

It's not a birthday party without balloons, and these balloons really pop. Hmm, maybe that wasn't a good choice of words.

Floral Cupcakes

LEVEL OF EASE: 2
ETW (ESTIMATED TIME OF WOW): 10 minutes per cupcake
RECOMMENDED SNACK: A cupcake, naturally

WHAT YOU'LL NEED

(per cupcake)
6 white pom-poms
1 red pom-pom
Small piece of floral foam
1 paper cupcake liner
1 foil cupcake liner

After waiting in line for more than a half hour at the Magnolia Bakery in New York City to buy a hummingbird cupcake, I knew I just had to make cupcakes out of flowers.

These floral cupcakes might not be edible, but they're a real treat for the eyes. Besides cheering up a table, they make great party favors or place-card holders. And you don't get that sugar crash afterward.

1 Cut a piece of floral foam that's ¾ inch high and 1½ inches in diameter.

2 Arrange the cupcake liners so that the foil liner rests inside the paper one.

3 Soak the floral foam in water, and place it in the foil liner.

4 Insert six white pom-poms into the top of the foam. With the floral cake, you placed the stems straight in. But for these cupcakes, you'll place the pom-poms using the Angled Method (see page 13). Cakes are flat; cupcakes have mounds.

5 Put the red pom-pom in the middle. That's the cherry on the icing.

1 Peel the petals off of a rose.

2 Spray one side of each petal with spray adhesive.

3 Apply the petals to the balloons, being sure to balance the petals around the balloon so one side doesn't become lopsided. Don't go overboard with the petals, or your balloon will sink from the extra weight.

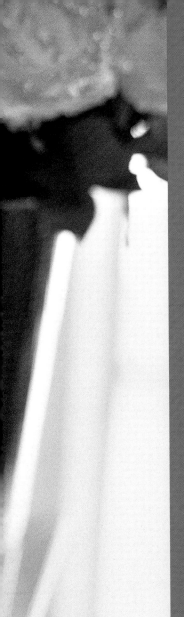

Chapter 2

Not the Same
Auld Lang Syne

I don't think I've ever made a New Year's resolution. Not that I'm perfect or anything. I just don't like kicking the year off with rules and restrictions. So if I had to make resolutions, I would resolve to eat more chocolate, spend more money, and be more incorrigible. That way I know I'll keep my promises. And I hope you'll resolve to try some of these New Year's floral projects.

Gift of Wine

WHAT YOU'LL NEED

4 large leaves, like aspidistra
Winter berries
Ivy
Raffia
Rubber band

Whenever I give a bottle of wine as a hostess gift, I have a hard time choosing, so I usually pick the one with the prettiest label. Because packaging is paramount in wine selection, I've started wrapping the bottles in lush leaves to add to the presentation.

LEVEL OF EASE: ③
ETW (ESTIMATED TIME OF WOW): 10 minutes
RECOMMENDED SNACK: Peanut M&M's

1 Wrap the first leaf around the wine bottle so that the leaf extends 3 inches above the tip of the bottle.

2   Cut the bottom of the leaf so it is level with the bottom of the bottle. Repeat with the rest of the leaves.

3   Use a rubber band to hold the leaves in place. Cover the rubber band with a raffia ribbon, and tie a bow.

4   Splay out the tips of the leaves to expose the top of the wine bottle.

5   Add a vine of ivy and a few berries for garnish.

Stemware Markers

LEVEL OF EASE: ②
ETW (ESTIMATED TIME OF WOW): 5 minutes
per marker
RECOMMENDED SNACK: Caramel popcorn

WHAT YOU'LL NEED

Flowers of different colors
Various leaves and foliage
Poster putty (ask for it at an art supply store)

At almost every party you go to nowadays, the host provides markers to help you identify which glass is yours. They can be made of lots of materials, including different colored beads or, as in the case of my relatives, blue masking tape with your name written on it. These markers made of fresh flowers are much more stylish.

1 Roll a piece of poster putty that's about 2 inches long. Cut a flower, leaving about 1 inch on the stem, and wrap the poster putty around it. Then wrap the poster putty around the base of the glass.

2 Continue to tuck more flowers into the poster putty so that eventually they cover the putty.

3 Place leaves over areas of the putty that are still exposed, and press down to secure them. Even out of water, most flowers will stay fresh for the length of your party. If they do begin to wilt, it will just be a subtle hint to your guests that it's time to go home.

Helpful Hint

To do this project, I like to purchase a pre-assembled, assorted bouquet at the supermarket. That way, I have a variety of flowers and colors to choose from.

Glitter Roses

LEVEL OF EASE: ①
ETW (ESTIMATED TIME OF WOW): 2 minutes per rose
RECOMMENDED SNACK: Pretzels

WHAT YOU'LL NEED

White roses
Silver glitter
Super 77 Spray Adhesive

I have a silver glitter sport coat that I used to wear to New Year's parties, but it blinded too many people so I had to retire it. These roses flecked with glitter are a much more tasteful way to add sparkle to the evening.

1 Spray the tips of the roses with adhesive. It's best to do this outside because the spray gets everywhere.

2 Pour some glitter into a plastic container. Dip each rose individually in the bowl so that the tips make contact with the glitter. Tap the stem against the rim of the bowl to shake off any excess. Arrange the roses in a silver wine bucket for maximum impact.

ও Florist Secret

Roses in florists' arrangements are so full, but the ones I buy never open up that much. How do the professionals do it? Believe it or not, many florists spread out the petals by hand. If the roses have come out of a cold case at the florist, let them sit out at room temperature (or even warmer) so they become more pliable. Start with the outer petals, peeling them back carefully. Stop when you get to the inner petals, which are more difficult to spread. Besides looking more lush, the open roses also take up two to four times as much surface area, so you need fewer flowers in your arrangement.

Chapter 3

Love,
Jonathan Fong–Style

Roses are red, violets are blue, come Valentine's Day, what do you do? For many, the pressure to be romantic on February 14 is so overwhelming that they become paralyzed with indecision. Some even avoid thinking about it until the last minute, and grab whatever's left at the florist or, worse yet, from the guy selling flowers at the freeway off-ramp. This year, plan ahead and make something special for your sweetheart. And here's good news for the men: one of the projects even uses power tools!

Chocolates and Flowers

LEVEL OF EASE: 4
ETW (ESTIMATED TIME OF WOW): 40 minutes
RECOMMENDED SNACK: Extra Hershey's Kisses

WHAT YOU'LL NEED

2 dozen red roses
21 Hershey's Kisses
21 floral stem wires
Ribbon

Flowers and chocolates go together, just like you and your loved one. This bouquet combines the two, with bunches of Hershey's Kisses cuddled between rose blooms. For your effort, you'll be showered with kisses—the real kind.

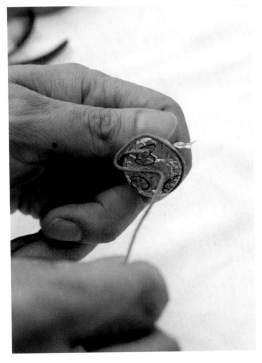

1 Attach the Hershey's Kisses to the ends of the floral wire, so each candy will have a "stem." I've chosen the Kisses with almonds, as they are wrapped in gold foil, which looks rich against the red roses. This step is the most difficult part of the project, because it can be a challenge to keep the Kiss on the wire. I experimented with various methods until I found a technique that really works. Begin with the wire flush against the bottom of the Kiss. Then run the wire in a circle around the base of the Kiss, and finish at the bottom of the candy, crossing over the end of the wire that was already there. The wires at the bottom act as a "seat" for the Kiss, and the loop keeps the Kiss from sliding off. The photo at the left shows how it should look.

2   Divide the Kisses into groups of three. They look more impressive that way. Otherwise, they can get lost in the bouquet. With twenty-one Kisses, you'll have seven groups of three.

3   Build the bouquet by placing the roses one stem at a time in your hand, grasping hold of each one. After every three or four roses, add one of the bunches of Hershey's Kisses so they are evenly interspaced between the roses. Keep rotating the bouquet in your hand to even out the roses and Kisses.

4   Tie a ribbon around the middle of the bouquet, where you've been holding it together. Just a simple knot will do. Finally, if any of the rose stems jut out farther than the others, cut the errant stems so they are all of a uniform length.

✿ *Florist Secret*

Always cut fresh stems at an angle, so that when the flower sits in a vase, the cut is not blocked by the surface of the glass. Also, the angle creates a larger area that is in contact with the water. As with cuts to our fingers, cuts to flowers "heal" and close up. Therefore, they need fresh cuts periodically so they keep drinking up the water.

Rose Ice Cubes

WHAT YOU'LL NEED

(per ice tray)
12 spray roses
12 twist ties
2 wooden skewers
1 ice tray
Floral tape

On Valentine's Day, you want everything to be perfect, right down to the tiniest detail. So instead of a wine bucket filled with common, everyday ice cubes, make a grand romantic gesture with these roses encased in ice. They'll melt any heart.

IS IT EDIBLE?

Most roses are indeed edible. However, many growers use pesticides on the roses, so I would avoid putting these ice cubes in drinks unless you're sure no chemicals were used. Just use the ice to cool the wine or champagne bottle.

1 To keep the roses submerged in the ice trays, we have to build a framework that will weigh them down. Cut the spray roses, leaving about 2 inches of stem, and use twist ties to attach the stems to the skewers.

2 Place the roses, which are attached to the skewers, upside down in the individual ice compartments of the tray.

3 Tape down the skewers at the ends of the ice tray to keep everything from floating when you add water. Your ice tray should look like the one in the photo.

4 Add water to the ice tray and freeze overnight.

5 When the ice is frozen, the skewers, stems, and twist ties will simply break off because the freezer makes them brittle. Loosen the ice from the tray and transfer it to an ice bucket.

Broadway's Bloopers

Look what happens when you put the rose buds in the ice tray without tying them down. They look very sad half in and half out of the ice, like roses afraid of commitment. Not good for Valentine's Day.

Sweetheart Rose Bouquet

LEVEL OF EASE: 2
ETW (ESTIMATED TIME OF WOW): 25 minutes
RECOMMENDED SNACK: Seedless grapes

WHAT YOU'LL NEED

2 flax leaves
1 bunch of spray or sweetheart roses
   (or any other flowers of your choice)
Stapler
Ribbon

Here's an even easier bouquet than the one made with Hershey's Kisses. You can also use other flowers besides roses. After all, it's the thought that counts.

1   Form a heart shape with the two flax leaves, as shown in the photo, and staple the leaves together at the bottom.

2   Arrange your flowers within the loops of the heart.

3   Tie a ribbon around the bouquet.

Diamond Life

LEVEL OF EASE: ②
ETW (ESTIMATED TIME OF WOW): 1 hour
(with some drying time for the paint)
RECOMMENDED SNACK: Onion rings

WHAT YOU'LL NEED

1 white rose
8-inch embroidery hoop
Wood glue
Silver metallic spray paint
Power drill

This whimsical project features a giant ring, with a white rose taking the place of the diamond. One tip, though: make sure you have some real jewelry on hand as well, or you may be sleeping on the couch.

1 An embroidery hoop has two pieces: an inner hoop that is solid, and an outer hoop that has an opening. Glue the two pieces of the hoop together, and let it dry overnight.

2 Drill a hole in the inner part of the embroidery hoop where there is an opening in the outer part.

3 Apply several coats of silver metallic spray paint in a well-ventilated area until the ring is a shiny silver.

Helpful Hint

Hang the ring with a piece of thread in a cardboard box. As you spray it, the ring will spin, and you'll spray all the sides at once.

4 Cut the stem of a white rose and insert it into the hole in the loop. It should fit snugly. Then cut off any excess stem.

✍ *Florist Secret:* How to Make a Valentine Wreath

FEATURING SUZANE LEMAY OF LES SCULPTURES VIVANTES IN
LOS ANGELES, CALIFORNIA

Suzane LeMay's talent and expertise in floral design have been recognized extensively by the Hollywood community, political figures, fashion designers, and a wide variety of personalities on the arts scene. For Valentine's Day, she recommends this heart-shaped wreath arrangement that can be given to men, because, as she says, "Guys love receiving flowers." I totally agree.

This project is easy with a heart-shaped floral foam wreath. While they're available at florist supply stores, it's easiest to order them online.

1 Soak the floral foam in water for at least fifteen minutes. Then place the floral foam on a towel, so the excess water will be absorbed as you work.

2 Cut stems of orchids and insert them around the foam.

3 Remove the foliage from eucalyptus branches, leaving the small berries. Insert the eucalyptus berries between the orchids to add texture to the arrangement.

4 Take about eight stalks of bear grass and create a heart by inserting the grass at the top of the heart, looping the stalks down on both sides of the heart and anchoring the ends to the foam with wire.

Chapter 4

Baby Showers

One by-product of the equality of the sexes is that now men are invited to baby showers. I've been to quite a few, and I am getting very good at that game in which everyone guesses the circumference of the expectant mother's waist by cutting a piece of string to the appropriate length. (The key is to underestimate. She's really not as wide as a hula hoop.)

The projects in this chapter will put everyone in a happy mood. Even the person who's sore about losing the game where you have to remember all the items under the baby blanket.

Umbrella Pendant

Instead of a centerpiece that sits on a table, this dramatic umbrella arrangement hangs over it. It's also perfect for bridal showers or any type of garden gathering.

1 We'll start with the flowers that will hang over the edge of the umbrella, like amaranthus or ivy. Attach them to the spokes of the umbrella with twist ties so they stay in place. What you'll have is a web of stems and twist ties attached to the spokes. It's not a pretty sight, but no one will see the inside of the umbrella.

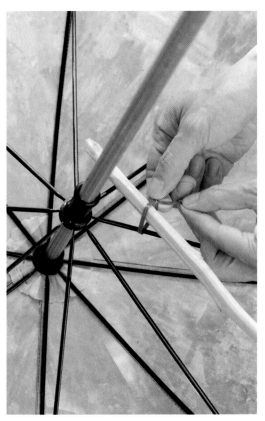

LEVEL OF EASE: 4
ETW (ESTIMATED TIME OF WOW): 45 minutes
RECOMMENDED SNACK: Carrot sticks

WHAT YOU'LL NEED

Various flowers, including hanging
   amaranthus or ivy
An umbrella with a hook handle
Twist ties

Helpful Hint

Find an umbrella that is colorful, rather than one that's black. For example, many children's umbrellas come in cheery pastels. I chose an umbrella with a reproduction of Monet's flowers on it, so that the flowers printed on the umbrella visually merge with the real flowers. Whatever umbrella you select, make sure it's the kind with a hook handle so you can hang it from a tree or from a hook in the ceiling.

2 Next, add other flowers that will peek over the edge of the umbrella. Remember that the flowers need to go to at least the edge of the umbrella to be seen. Use twist ties to secure these new flowers to the "web of stems" from step 1.

3 When the umbrella starts getting heavy from all the flowers, hook it on the tree so you don't have to worry about lifting it later. When the umbrella gets heavy, the web of stems is dense enough that you can now add additional flowers just by tucking subsequent flowers into the "web." They'll stay in place without being tied down. Work around the entire umbrella so that the flowers are balanced and not concentrated on one side.

HOW LONG WILL IT LAST?

Since none of the stems have a water source, you may be wondering how long this arrangement will last. Good news. It will not only look beautiful for the entire day but will continue to be presentable long after. When we finished photographing this arrangement for the book, I set it out in the front yard, and neighbors marveled at it for three days before the flowers needed to be taken down.

Baby Bottle Vases

What adorable bud vases these pastel baby bottles make. The nipple even helps hold the stem steady. And get this: the bottles were made by Gerber, and I used Gerber daisies. It was meant to be!

1 Cut the tip off the nipple of the baby bottle.

2 Fill the bottle with water.

3 Insert the daisy into the bottle through the nipple.

ꙮ Florist Secret

Flowers can travel for days without water after they're harvested from the fields, so they might be a little wilted when they arrive at the florist. Or you may have flowers at home that have become prematurely droopy. They can be resuscitated, though. Submerge them—blooms and all—in water for several hours, let them drink up the water, and they'll be as good as new.

LEVEL OF EASE: 1
ETW (ESTIMATED TIME OF WOW): 2 minutes per bottle
RECOMMENDED SNACK: A Pop-Tart

Baby Blocks

LEVEL OF EASE: 4
ETW (ESTIMATED TIME OF WOW): 45 minutes per block
RECOMMENDED SNACK: A bowl of ice cream

WHAT YOU'LL NEED

Pom-poms of at least three different colors (approx. 96 pom-poms per block; pom-poms come in bunches of hundreds)
1 brick of floral foam (makes 3 blocks)

I needed to make a table decoration for a baby shower and conceived this idea for baby blocks made of flowers. The delivery was pretty painless, too.

1 Cut the brick of floral foam into three pieces, using the lines that are already embossed on the foam to guide you. Then cut about an inch off each end to form a cube. Each brick of floral foam yields three cubes.

2 After soaking the foam in water, work with one side at a time. Insert one color of pom-poms around the edge to form a square. Use the Straight-in Method (see page 13).

3 Then fill the inside of the square with a flower of a contrasting color. Either fill it in with a solid shape, or create simple letters like C, O, and T. (The pom-poms are too large to attempt more complex letters like M or R.)

4 When you work with subsequent sides of the cube, repeat the process. Be sure to work to the very edge of each side so that the adjacent sides meet without any gaps.

Chapter 5

Spring Fling

When I lived in Boston, the promise of spring was what got me through the winters. The thought of milder days and sun-kissed flower blossoms was a welcome mental retreat while I trudged down Commonwealth Avenue dressed like an Eskimo. No matter that spring only lasted a week before the muggy summer weather took over.

We all feel happier in the spring. The days start to get longer, and the extra sunshine does wonders for our moods. (It's a scientific fact.) The floral arrangements in this chapter epitomize the cheery nature of the season, as you can't make them without having a big smile on your face.

What's Up, Bunny?

LEVEL OF EASE: ⑤
ETW (ESTIMATED TIME OF WOW): 1½ hours
RECOMMENDED SNACK: Animal crackers

This bunny was one of the first floral arrangements I ever made. I created it for an Easter dinner, and of course it was a big hit. It's another testament to the wonders of floral foam. You can make anything with the stuff! The bunny would also be a great centerpiece for a baby shower, birthday party, or celebration when one of your friends becomes a Playboy bunny.

WHAT YOU'LL NEED

60 (approx.) white carnations
2 large red tea leaves
2 pink Gerber daisies
1 red pom-pom
1 China mum
Twigs
2 bricks of floral foam
3 wooden skewers
Large platter

1 First, carve one brick of floral foam into an oval, which will be the bunny's body. Soak it in water and place the body on the large platter. Then cut the second floral foam brick in half, and carve an oval out of a half-brick to create the head. (Don't forget to soak the head in water.)

2 Using the wooden skewers, attach the head to the body. The head should rest toward the front of the body, not directly on top of it. I recommend three skewers because you need that many to stabilize the head. With one or two skewers, the head would pivot or, worse, fall off. We don't want a headless bunny. Children would cry.

3 The white carnations will be the bunny's fur. Starting at the bottom of the body, work your way up, inserting carnations into the floral foam using the Angled Method (see page 13). After you're finished with the body, you can move on to the head. At this point, your bunny looks like a big white blob. Don't worry, it'll look like the real thing soon enough.

4 Gerber daisies make great eyes for the bunny. The center of the daisy looks like the eyeball, and the petals act like eyelashes. (I'm not sure if bunnies have eyelashes, but this is not a time to be anatomically correct.) You may need to remove a carnation or two to make room for the daisy.

5 Underneath the eyes, insert a red pom-pom for the nose. Then place two twigs on either side of the nose for whiskers.

6 All right, now your creation looks like a mutant dog. But ears will make it a bunny, and red tea leaves have the right shape and color. Just stick the stem of each leaf into the top of the head, squeezing past the carnations into the floral foam until they are secure. See, it's a bunny!

7 On the bunny's behind, place a big, bushy China mum for the tail. Again, you may need to remove one or two carnations to fit the tail.

8 Finally, tuck four white carnations underneath the entire body where the feet would go. A word of caution: if you make two of these arrangements, don't place them together or they might multiply.

Basket Case

WHAT YOU'LL NEED

2 calla lilies
20 (approx.) roses
8 (approx.) chrysanthemums
3 (approx.) Gerber daisies
1 brick of floral foam
1 small planter or pot
1 long stick
Ribbon
Twist tie

I often make these "basket" arrangements as gifts for friends. They're simple, but they look elegant and expensive. I love how the calla lilies hook together on top to form a handle for the basket, which is just a regular planter.

Helpful Hint

To get the calla lilies to curve without breaking, leave them out of water for a few hours so the stems become rubbery. Then bend them slowly.

1 Carve the wet floral foam to fit into the pot. You can use smaller pieces of the foam to wedge the foam in for a tighter fit.

2 Insert the calla lilies into the foam at an angle, so that the two sides of the handle bow out before they join together at the top.

Instead of calla lilies, you can make a beautiful basket "handle" by using curly willow and ivy. Start with two or three strands of curly willow, inserting the bottom ends into one side of the floral foam. Then loop the curly willow over the planter to create the handle, securing the tips to the other side of the floral foam with some greening pins (the tips of the curly willow are not stiff enough to insert into the floral foam). Finally, wrap some ivy around the curly willow to give it color and dimension.

3 Place a stick in the middle of the floral foam, and tie the calla lilies to it at the top with the twist tie.

4 Begin adding flowers to the floral foam, starting at the bottom and working your way up. Insert the stems using the Angled Method (see page 13) so you get a dome shape.

5 Cover the twist tie by tying a bow around it.

Broadway's Bloopers

Remember that the calla lilies need to be inserted at an angle so the "handle" of the basket curves out and then in for a nice circular shape. Otherwise, the shape of the handle is a thin triangle, which you can see is not as attractive.

Warhol Daisies

WHAT YOU'LL NEED

4 different colors of spray roses, approx. 20 each
4 Gerber daisies of different colors
1 acrylic box frame, 8½ x 11 inches
1 brick of floral foam, plus a little extra
Floral tape
Tabletop display easel

Everyone knows I'm a big Warhol fan, and this live take on his Gerber daisy silkscreens is a sunny tribute.

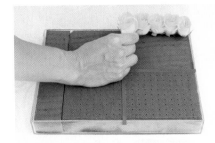

1 Carve the floral foam to fit into the acrylic box frame. Of course, discard the cardboard part of the frame first. Using floral tape, bisect the frame horizontally and vertically to create four quadrants. (Boy, I haven't used the word "bisect" since high school.) This also helps keep the foam in place later when you're putting the arrangement on an easel.

2 In each quadrant, line up the spray roses using the Straight-in Method (see page 13). Depending on the size of the roses, you'll use about four rows of five roses per quadrant. However, leave a space in the middle where you'll be putting the Gerber daisy.

3 Insert a Gerber daisy in the middle of each quadrant. Be sure to select a color that contrasts with the color of the surrounding roses. Place the entire frame on the desktop easel, and enjoy your fifteen minutes of fame.

Florist Secret: How to Make a Vase-within-a-Vase Arrangement

FEATURING WALTER NICOLAS OF NICOLAS FLOWERS & EVENTS IN BEVERLY HILLS, CALIFORNIA

Window shopping on famed Rodeo Drive in Beverly Hills one afternoon, I noticed that in store after store, the floral displays were exquisite. And every time I asked who did the flowers, the salespeople said, "Walter Nicolas." Despite his busy schedule, Walter made time to demonstrate for us how to make a vase-within-a-vase arrangement. He uses kumquats in this project for a spring feel, but you can vary what you put between the vases depending on the occasion—for example, cranberries during the holidays, sand for a beach party, or candy corn for Halloween.

1 You'll need two vases, one smaller than the other. In the inner vase, anchor a floral frog with some floral adhesive putty. A floral frog is a heavy round disk with many spikes, used to hold floral stems in place. Then fill the inner vase with water.

2 Fill the area between the two vases with kumquats, placing them individually by hand rather than just pouring them in, so that the space is filled in solidly.

3 Start with the largest blooms, which are the hydrangeas. Cut the stems so the bottom is held by the floral frog and the hydrangea blossoms spill over the rim of the outer vase.

4 Follow with additional flowers, like Siberia lilies, bouvardia, white lilac, and ranunculus, until the flowers take on a full, rounded shape. When you're finished, it looks like the flowers are growing out of a bowl of kumquats. It's both playful and elegant.

Chapter 6

Gung Hay Fat Choy

The greeting that's heard during Chinese New Year, "Gung hay fat choy," doesn't really mean "Happy New Year." It literally translates as "Happiness and good fortune." I guess we Chinese are much more specific about what we want. To go with the good fortune sentiment, we also exchange envelopes filled with dollar bills as tokens of hope for prosperity. I'm not sure if you'll get good fortune by doing these festive, Asian-inspired arrangements, but you'll certainly get a lot of happiness.

Chinese Take-Out

LEVEL OF EASE: ③
ETW (ESTIMATED TIME OF WOW): 1 hour
RECOMMENDED SNACK: Potato salad (you'll see why)

WHAT YOU'LL NEED

One each from column A:
1 ready-made bouquet from a supermarket
1 plain, white take-out container, quart size
1 plastic tub container, pint size
Decorative paper
Super 77 Spray Adhesive
½ brick of floral foam
Chopsticks
Brayer (a roller for applying pressure that helps two
   surfaces adhere; buy one at any art supply store)

I once made 120 of these arrangements as centerpieces for a charity gala. I constructed each of the take-out boxes by hand, covering them with Chinese brocade fabric. Here I've used decorative paper instead because it's much easier to work with. The only problem with this arrangement is that after thirty minutes, you're hungry to make another one.

1 The easiest way to get a take-out container is to ask your local Chinese restaurant for an extra one. Don't try to wash an old one; they tend to get oily. Disassemble the take-out container by removing the wire handle so that the container becomes flat. Spray the side of the container that faces out with some Super 77, and place the sticky side onto the back side of your decorative paper. Roll a brayer over the container to make sure the two elements adhere thoroughly.

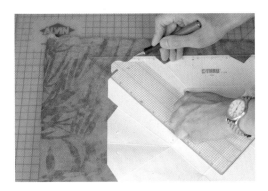

2 Using an X-Acto knife and a straight edge, trim the excess paper around the take-out container. Most of the sides are straight, so it's easy, but you'll have to be a little more careful around the curved parts of the container. You'll notice that there are eight holes in the container where the wire handle was attached. Be sure to poke a large hole through them with the X-Acto, as you'll need these holes to put everything back together.

3 Now fold the container back together. It's easy because the pre-folded container will want to go back to its original shape. Line up the holes where the wire handle used to be and reattach the handle. If you're in a hurry, many gift stores also sell take-out containers wrapped in satin, or plastic ones in colorful shades, so you can just buy those and skip these first steps.

4 Buy a pint of potato salad at the deli counter, eat the potato salad, and wash the plastic tub. The tub will fit perfectly into the take-out container. Carve the floral foam to fit the tub. Dunk the foam in water, and place it in the tub. Don't put the foam directly into the take-out container; the water might leak and ruin the paper that's wrapped around it.

5 The easiest way to fill the container with flowers is to buy a large, pre-assembled bouquet at the supermarket. Insert the flowers around the edges first, and then fill in the middle, always using the Angled Method (see page 13) to create a domed shape.

6 For a fun finishing touch, insert a pair of chopsticks into the foam. It gives the arrangement additional height and drama.

Broadway's Bloopers

Besides not covering the container, there are a few common mistakes here. First is that the stems are showing, because the flowers were not inserted at an angle to hide the stems. Also, the chopsticks are too short, so they're lost in the arrangement. Remember to use long chopsticks rather than the short wooden ones that come with take-out food.

Tea Garden

Suddenly, tea is the new coffee. Because tea is so in, I'm finding the most beautiful teapots in stores. The one here is from the Hong Kong Café, the restaurant my parents used to own. With just a handful of bright flowers, you have an instant arrangement.

LEVEL OF EASE: ❶

ETW (ESTIMATED TIME OF WOW): 3 minutes

RECOMMENDED SNACK: Fortune cookie

1 Cut the stems so they are shorter than the depth of the teapot.

2 Place the flowers in the teapot in a rounded shape.

Red Lantern

WHAT YOU'LL NEED

2 calla lilies
Bamboo leaves
1 paper lantern
1 bud vase

1 Open up the paper lantern and slip a bud vase through the top opening.

2 Place calla lilies and bamboo in the bud vase.

Helpful Hint

You can use other flowers in the lantern, but think simple. Don't go overboard on the number of flowers you choose or use too many varieties. A lush garden bouquet would not look right in the lantern.

LEVEL OF EASE: ①
ETW (ESTIMATED TIME OF WOW): 3 minutes
RECOMMENDED SNACK: Rice cracker trail mix

I love the simplicity of this arrangement. It's so zen.

Florist Secret: How to Pot an Orchid

FEATURING ROMAN SACKE OF KYTKA FLORAL DESIGN IN
LOS ANGELES, CALIFORNIA

Potted orchids are one of my favorite gifts to give because they bloom for several months, and even people with the brownest thumbs can keep them alive. I've purchased many of these orchid gifts from Kytka Floral Design, so Roman Sacke, whose clients include royalty (and I'm not talking about myself), showed me how anyone can take store-bought orchids and turn them into professional arrangements.

1 Keep the orchids in their plastic container and soak the roots in water for at least ten minutes.

2 Ball up old newspapers and place them on the bottom of a piece of decorative pottery. The newspapers prop up the orchid containers and absorb run-off water.

3 Position one or two orchids (still in their plastic containers) in the decorative pottery, depending on how large it is. You can also add a house plant, or a smaller orchid, to fill out your arrangement.

4 Remove the plain stick that came with the orchids and replace it with a bamboo pole or similar piece of decorative wood. Tie the orchid to the bamboo with a piece of raffia.

5 Insert curly willow into the orchid pots and wrap the willow around the bamboo.

6 Soak sheet moss in water and squeeze out the excess moisture. Roll the wet moss into little mounds and cover the top of the plastic container(s) with these little "hills and valleys." The moss will also straighten out the bamboo and willow into an upright position.

Chapter 7

Mum's the Word

It's hard shopping for mothers, isn't it? They seem to have everything. So on Mother's Day, it's nearly impossible to come up with that one spectacular, expensive-looking present that shows how much you love her. Gift idea number one is a copy of one of my books. She'll instantly put you at the top of the will for that. And here are three more ideas that will guarantee you a place in her good graces. If you have siblings, these projects will make them insane with resentment and jealousy. And isn't that what this day is all about?

Mother's Day Keepsake

LEVEL OF EASE: ③
ETW (ESTIMATED TIME OF WOW): 1½ hours
RECOMMENDED SNACK: Peanut brittle

WHAT YOU'LL NEED

Bouquet of 2 dozen roses from
     a supermarket or other store
1 or 2 contrasting flowers to
     add texture
Leaves
Upholstered keepsake box
Plastic liner
1 brick of floral foam

I came upon this idea when I was at Ross Dress for Less and saw a large variety
of upholstered keepsake boxes for less than $10 each. They looked so elegant,
and I knew that they would be the perfect vessel for some store-bought roses.

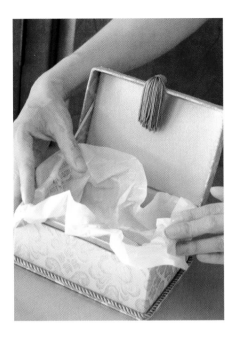

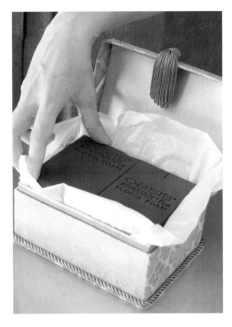

1   You'll want to protect the keep-sake box so it can be used again. Line the box with plastic liner. You don't have to buy anything special for this purpose. I just cut off the corner of a kitchen trash bag.

2   Carve your floral foam to fit into the container, soak it in water, and place it in the plastic. Pulling up the plastic to keep it taut, cut off any excess plastic liner. Be careful as you're cutting that you don't cut the little ribbon that holds up the box lid.

3   As tempting as it may be to start with the roses, I like to use the contrasting flowers first, like the purple flowers in the photo. Why? Because the roses will go on top and partially cover them. If you put the roses in first, the bushy flowers might cover them later.

4   Now you can put in the roses. For the ones in the front, use the Angled Method (see page 13), and be sure to angle them forward so they face front. Again, that way you will have a more rounded shape. Then place some random leaves between the roses to break up the color and add a finishing texture to the whole arrangement. You can use the leaves that come with your rose bouquet, or look in your backyard for ivy or other foliage. Free is good.

A LOVEABLE IDEA

Place a little "I love you" note at the bottom of the arrangement, underneath the plastic, so when Mom throws away the flowers after a week or so, she'll find the hidden sentiment.

Family Tree

LEVEL OF EASE: 3
ETW (ESTIMATED TIME OF WOW): 3 hours
RECOMMENDED SNACK: A cup of herbal tea

WHAT YOU'LL NEED

3 artificial silver dollar branches
Rocks
Planter
1 brick of dry floral foam
Photographs of family members
Glue stick

For once, the whole family can be together, at least on the family tree.

1 Cut pieces of foam to place in the planter.

2 Insert the dollar plant stems in the foam.

3 Cover the foam with rocks.

4 Splay out the branches to form a tree.

5 Glue photos of family members onto the silver dollars, with the older members on top, and the young ones (like you and me) at the bottom.

Floral Photo Frame

WHAT YOU'LL NEED

Small silk flowers, like ranunculus or
    hydrangea, that can be cut into smaller buds
1 brick of dry floral foam
1 wooden photo frame
Hot glue gun

The silk flowers surrounding this photo frame give it an
heirloom quality.

2 Cut the buds off the
silk flower stem.

1 Cut the dry foam into
½-inch thick pieces that
cover the wooden part
of the frame. Then, using
a hot glue gun, attach
the foam to the frame.
Press down on the foam
until the glue sets so you
have a nice, secure hold.

3 Insert silk flowers
into the foam.

AND SOMETHING FOR DAD

Sure, dads get bored with ties for
Father's Day. But wrap a tie around a
bouquet of calla lilies, and you've got
a pretty nifty gift.

Florist Secret: How to Make a Bouquet

FEATURING THE FLORAL DESIGNERS AT EFFUSIVE FLOWERS, LOS ANGELES, CALIFORNIA

While I've made plenty of bouquets by bunching flowers together with a ribbon, I had never made a proper one until my friends at Effusive Flowers showed me how.

1 Put one or two flowers together for the center of your bouquet and wrap them with stem wrap tape (see page 12). Then add one or two stems at a time around this center, and wrap these increments with the tape.

2 Add another flower or, as in the case of this bouquet, some berries, and tape them. Continue wrapping the stems until there is a band of tape that is the width of your hand.

3 Next, wrap leaves around the tape handle, and cover these leaves with more stem wrap tape.

4 Wrap ribbon around the bouquet to hide all the tape. Fold the end of the ribbon over so you get a clean edge, and insert eight to ten straight pins to secure the ribbon (pins with a decorative element, like faux pearl, on the end look nice).

Chapter 8

America the Beautiful

When I was a kid, the Fourth of July was a big deal. It was one of the few holidays when my family's Chinese restaurant closed, so we got to act like a typical all-American family, eating hot dogs and hamburgers, lighting our "safe and sane" sparklers, and watching the city's fireworks. It was a red-letter (make that red-white-and-blue-letter) day. As I've gotten older, I still treasure those memories. Now these patriotic floral arrangements are part of my new Independence Day tradition. I hope they'll become part of your family's, too.

Floral Fireworks

WHAT YOU'LL NEED

2 agapanthus stems
2 spider mums
Moss
Container
2 bricks of floral foam
Greening pins
Miniature toy cars

In my neighborhood, agapanthus grow like weeds in July. While walking my dog, Broadway, I couldn't help noticing how much they look like fireworks. It's as though they bloom just in time to celebrate the Fourth. Taking advantage of their unique shape, I created this whimsical fireworks tableau. It reminds me of when my dad would drive us to the city park, and we'd lie on the hood of the car and look up at the fireworks in the sky.

1 You can choose any type of container, but I found a red, white, and blue one at the crafts store, so how could I resist? Cut the floral foam to fit into the container, soak the foam in water, and place the pieces in the container. If you're using a container that can leak, line it with plastic first.

2 For the grass in this idyllic scene, moss does the trick. Using greening pins, anchor the pieces of moss into the foam at the edge of the container. You don't want to fill the middle with moss yet because we still have to install the "fireworks."

3 Cut the two agapanthus stems to different heights, and insert them in the foam at various angles, so it looks like the fireworks are crisscrossing. Next, place two spider mums in the foam. I recommend spider mums because they also look like fireworks, especially if you pluck off some of the petals so they're more sparse.

4 Finish your lawn by placing moss on the remainder of the floral foam, around the stems of the agapanthus and spider mums. Then park the cars on the grass. If you happen to have little people, that would be even funnier.

Drinking Straw Arrangement

LEVEL OF EASE: ②
ETW (ESTIMATED TIME OF WOW): 15 minutes
RECOMMENDED SNACK: Red Vines licorice sticks

WHAT YOU'LL NEED

Red and white
  Gerber daisies
30 (approx.) red and blue
  flexi-straws
1 tumbler
1 rubber band
1 red or blue ribbon

This colorful vase is one of my most popular projects. Here I've customized it for Independence Day with red and blue straws. People always think the straws are glued on the tumbler, but they're just held in place by a rubber band.

1 Place a rubber band around the middle of a tumbler. Make sure that the tumbler is as straight up and down as possible, with little or no flare. That way, the straws will line up straight. Slide the straws between the glass and the rubber band. Alternate colors randomly.

2 Hide the rubber band by tying a ribbon around it.

3 Bend the flexi-straws to give your vase some extra pizzazz. If your straws aren't the bendable type, that's fine, too.

Helpful Hint

Both glass and plastic vases get a white, filmy residue where the water sits. To clean the vase so it's sparkling again, use a solution of vinegar and water.

Broadway's Bloopers

The straws are going haywire here. Why? Because the tumbler has too much of a flare to it. The straws can't line up straight, so they start twisting around. Then it's drinking straw anarchy.

Wave the Flag

WHAT YOU'LL NEED

36 (approx.) red pom-poms
36 (approx.) white pom-poms
12 (approx.) blue mums
8½ x 11 acrylic box frame
1½ bricks of floral foam
1 tabletop display easel

Similar in method to the Warhol Daisies (see page 48), this project will have you singing the Star-Spangled Banner, complete with the high notes.

1 Carve the floral foam to fit into the acrylic frame. Soak the foam and insert it into the frame.

2 Like the Warhol arrangement, this one has four quadrants. In the upper-left quadrant, line up three rows of blue mums, using the Straight-in Method (see page 13). These are the stars.

3 In the upper-right quadrant, alternate rows of red and white pom-poms.

4 The bottom half of the frame comprises the rest of the flag, so continue alternating rows of red and white pom-poms until you're finished.

5 Either display it flat on the table, or place it on a tabletop easel.

Florist Secret: How to Make a Leaf-lined Arrangement

FEATURING ELIZABETH BAILEY OF BARRINGTON FLOWERS IN
BRENTWOOD, CALIFORNIA

I first became aware of Barrington Flowers when I saw their
stunning work at a design house showcase. I love how they use
just a few elements in unusual combinations to create magic.
Here, owner Elizabeth Bailey shows how to make a vase
arrangement that's lined with leaves, which hide the unsightly
stems and completely transform the glass vase.

1 Select any leaf with interesting stripes or colors. Elizabeth notes that the most common house-plants have beautiful (and free) leaves you can use. If you have a tall vase, line the leaves straight up and down. If you have a shorter vase, like the one in the photo, roll the leaves and place them on their sides.

2 Roll up some curly willow and place it in the vase to help the leaves stand up. If the leaves are oversized, trim them so they line up with the top of the vase.

3 Create a grid of floral tape (see page 12) across the top of the vase. This will help the flowers that you insert later stay in place. Tape the lip of the vase to secure the floral tape grid. Now add water to the vase. You'll notice that the water magnifies everything, so the leaves look even more brilliant.

4 Insert the flowers in clusters, so that all the roses are together, all the tulips are together, all the rolled up leaves, etc. This creates a cleaner arrangement than one in which the flowers are mixed. Choosing a monochromatic color scheme also helps.

Chapter 9

New Fall Classics

Why do I love fall? Because it starts around my birthday (October 5) and keeps getting better from there. The new television shows debut. We get an extra hour of sleep when daylight saving time ends. I get to turn on the heater full blast. And it's party after party, from Halloween get-togethers to tailgate barbecues to Thanksgiving potlucks. I think that extra hour of sleep really boosts creativity, because the following fall floral projects are some of my favorites. Can someone pass the floral turkey, please?

Attack of the Killer Centerpiece

LEVEL OF EASE: ③
ETW (ESTIMATED TIME OF WOW): 1½ hours
RECOMMENDED SNACK: Gummi worms

WHAT YOU'LL NEED

2 proteas
40 (approx.) brown mums
8 stems of pussy willow
6-inch plastic plate
Florist tape
1 brick of floral foam

I get a kick out of Halloween. I always put on my favorite costume, which is khakis, a button-down shirt, and a Gap employee name tag, and I go around asking people if they need help finding a size. Scary! Now, people don't usually associate Halloween with flowers, but as you can see in this chapter, they can add a lot to the festivities.

This giant spider is inspired by those horror movies in which giant mutant insects wreak havoc on a private island and munch on actresses like the pre-*Dynasty* Joan Collins. It would be a great centerpiece at a Halloween party (the food would fit under the legs). Or scar your children for life by putting this on their bed so it's the first thing they see when they wake up. Ah, good times.

1 Round the edges of the brick of floral foam so it's more of an oval. Soak it in water, and place it on top of the plastic plate. The plate will give the arrangement stability so you can easily carry the spider around to freak people out. Secure the foam onto the plate with the florist tape, as I've shown in the photograph.

2 Pussy willow makes perfect legs for the spider because the wooly bumps make the spider legs even more creepy. Cut the ends of the pieces of pussy willow so that the length of each one is about 2½ feet. Then bend the pussy willow in half until it cracks a little, but not so much that you break it. Now the leg is bent like a real spider's. Stick four legs on each side of the "body." They should be angled so that the legs are splayed out, rather than facing in just two directions.

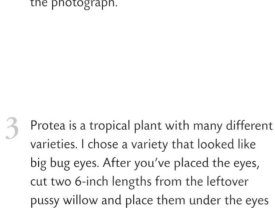

3 Protea is a tropical plant with many different varieties. I chose a variety that looked like big bug eyes. After you've placed the eyes, cut two 6-inch lengths from the leftover pussy willow and place them under the eyes as fangs. Then fill the body with mums as the "hair." You now have a new family pet.

OTHER OPTIONS

If you can't find pussy willow, try horsetail or long, thin tree branches. And if protea isn't available in your local stores, any type of flower or vegetation that can pass as eyes will work—daisies, pin cushions, even mushrooms!

Bubbly Cauldron

LEVEL OF EASE: 2
ETW (ESTIMATED TIME OF WOW): 20 minutes
RECOMMENDED SNACK: Sweet Tarts

WHAT YOU'LL NEED

1 mother-in-law's tongue plant
Flame-colored flowers or foliage
1 plastic cauldron
Dry ice
Plastic or styrofoam cup

Bubble, bubble, toil and trouble! Actually, this project entails little toil or trouble. And the dry ice creates a nice special effect.

1 Place the mother-in-law's tongue in the plastic cauldron. (I know it's a horrible name, but I didn't make it up.) The twisting tendrils of the plant look like fumes coming from the cauldron.

2 Create smoke by placing some dry ice in a cup; nestle the cup between the leaves and the rim of the cauldron, letting it sit in the soil. (The dry ice won't hurt the plant.) Fill the cup with warm water to create smoky fog. Place the cup as high as possible so the smoke spills over the cauldron; prop it up with paper towels or pieces of cardboard, if necessary.

Helpful Hint

Place a few cups of dry ice behind the cauldron as well, so fog spreads everywhere. The hotter the water, the more fog you'll produce.

3 Underneath the cauldron, place dahlias or other red and orange foliage that resembles flames.

ABOUT DRY ICE

When looking for dry ice, start at the supermarket. Mine sells it in packs. Or check the yellow pages under "ice." The packs come with special instructions for handling; be sure to read them carefully. Remind your kids that dry ice is not a toy. Wear protective gloves, because dry ice is extremely cold and should not make direct contact with your skin.

Halloween Pumpkin

WHAT YOU'LL NEED

Autumn-colored flowers
    like alstroemeria
Rosewood pumpkin, or a
    plastic or hollowed-out
    fresh pumpkin
Plastic cup

For those of you with less macabre sensibilities, here's a simple project using exotic rosewood pumpkins. The Resource Directory at the back of the book tells you where to buy these hand-carved pumpkins.

1 Place a plastic cup in the pumpkin and fill it with water.

2 Fill the pumpkin with flowers so the stems sit in the cup.

3 If the pumpkin has a lid, place it right on top of the flowers.

LEVEL OF EASE: 1
ETW (ESTIMATED TIME OF WOW): 2 minutes
RECOMMENDED SNACK: Pumpkin seeds

Florist Secret

Spray the leaves of your arrangements and houseplants with a "leaf shine" product (there are many brands). It gets rid of hard water stains and dulling so the leaves look positively radiant.

Gobble Gobble

LEVEL OF EASE: 3
ETW (ESTIMATED TIME OF WOW): 1½ hours
RECOMMENDED SNACK: Pecan pie

WHAT YOU'LL NEED

40 (approx.) brown or orange mums
1 bird of paradise
1 or 2 palm fronds
10 foxtails
1 brick of floral foam
Large platter

This floral turkey centerpiece reminds me of a float in the Rose Parade. It certainly puts people in the Thanksgiving spirit. After demonstrating it on my website, I got a lot of photographs from people who tried it themselves and gave it their own spin. And why not? There are countless ways to prepare a turkey.

1   Carve the floral foam so it's an oval shape, like the body of the spider on page 77. It should look like a green turkey breast. Soak it in water and place it on the platter.

2   Start at the bottom of the foam and work up, inserting the mums using the Angled Method (see page 13) to create a domed shape for the turkey's body.

3 At the back of the body, insert a palm frond. My example in the photograph actually uses two palm fronds because they were very thin; use your judgment about how many you'll need. At this point, your centerpiece will look more like a pineapple than a turkey, but don't worry. It will look like a turkey soon enough.

4 To give the feathers an added dimension, intersperse foxtails between the spokes of the palm frond. You can buy dried foxtails easily at this time of year in the supermarket or crafts store.

5 It's the bird of paradise that makes the turkey. Cut the flower so the stem is about 15 inches long, and insert it at the front of the body, pushing aside a few mums to fit the stem in. I get the drumstick!

Broadway's Bloopers

As I said, there are a lot of ways to make a turkey. This blooper, created by my photographer, Jessica Boone, shows what one looks like with different flowers. Sure, a bird of paradise looks more like a turkey head than the ginger stalk she used, and the palm frond needs to be wider to have that "turkiness," but I do love the creativity of this arrangement. It's definitely a modern art version of Mr. Gobble. So don't be ashamed of your bloopers! Just say they were meant to be that way.

Three-in-One Herb Centerpiece

WHAT YOU'LL NEED

9–12 pre-planted herbs, 4-inch size
1 basket (approx. 10 x 14 inches and
    4 inches deep)
9–12 pieces of 12-inch-square fabric, in
    assorted fall colors/patterns
1 large cloth napkin or placemat
A supply of raffia ribbon
Assorted plastic food containers

I created this arrangement for a Thanksgiving makeover show on the USA Network. It's an ingenious herb garden that (1) functions as a centerpiece or hostess gift, (2) comes apart for individual party favors, and (3) hides plastic containers for Thanksgiving leftovers!

1 Wrap each container of herbs in a piece of fabric, tying the fabric on with a raffia ribbon.

2 Cover the bottom of the basket by lining it with the plastic food containers.

3 Hide the containers with the large napkin or placemat.

4 Place the herbs on top of the covered plastic containers.

Asparagus Vase

LEVEL OF EASE: 2
ETW (ESTIMATED TIME OF WOW): 20 minutes
RECOMMENDED SNACK: Potato chips

WHAT YOU'LL NEED

20 (approx.) asparagus spears
1 bunch of sunflowers
1 tumbler
1 rubber band
2 pieces of corn silk
1 raffia ribbon

Here's a variation of the drinking straw arrangement from page 70, with asparagus spears instead of straws. The sunflowers are a bright complement to the asparagus.

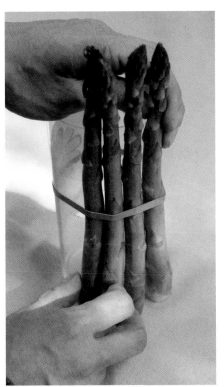

1   Place a rubber band around the middle of the tumbler.

2   Insert asparagus spears between the rubber band and the tumbler.

3   Hide the rubber band with the two pieces of corn silk, and secure them with a raffia ribbon.

4   Place the sunflowers and water in the tumbler.

✑ *Florist Secret*

Large-stemmed flowers like sunflowers break down quickly in water, creating bacteria and muddiness. An easy way to change the water without disturbing your flowers is to place the entire arrangement in the sink and let the water run for several minutes with the flowers still in the vase. Also, put a drop of bleach in the water to kill bacteria.

Chapter 10

Holiday Greetings

Living in Southern California, where it's in the upper 70s during December, it's hard to get into the holiday spirit. There are no sensory cues like the chill of snow or the smell of firewood to wake up our inner Kris Kringle. So I put on all my Christmas CDs, take out the aluminum tree I bought on eBay, and decorate the house. Before long I'm in a "ho ho ho" mood. I like to decorate for the holidays just before Thanksgiving and leave everything up until mid-January, so I have two full months to enjoy it. An integral part of the décor, of course, is flowers.

Free-Standing Ornament

LEVEL OF EASE: ⑤
ETW (ESTIMATED TIME OF WOW): 1 hour
RECOMMENDED SNACK: Egg nog

WHAT YOU'LL NEED

40 (approx.) yellow pom-poms
5 red pom-poms
1 pine bough, artificial or real
1 banana stand
⅓ brick of floral foam
Fishing line
Green twist ties
Red ribbon
1 pack of ten battery-operated
   miniature lights

Even if you don't have a tree, you can still create this floral ornament because it hangs on its own branch. It looks festive on a mantel or desk, and it even lights up, thanks to a short string of battery-operated lights.

1 Cut a small ball out of the floral foam. A diameter of 3 inches or less is preferable, because you don't want a humongous ornament. Just keep shaving the foam a little at a time until you get a nice sphere shape.

2 Next, circle fishing line around the floral foam ball and tie a knot. Then dunk the whole thing in water. Fishing line is perfect for this project because it is durable even when wet, and it's practically invisible.

3 Now let's move on to the branch. Wrap the pine bough around the banana stand, holding it in place with the twist ties. Be sure to cover the entire length of the banana stand with pine.

4 Tuck a piece of red ribbon underneath the fishing wire, then tie the ribbon around the hook of the banana stand. Be careful not to jiggle the ball around at this point, because the fishing line will dig into the foam. If it cuts into the foam too much, it might slice it in half.

5 I've decorated the foam with yellow pom-poms because they are a small, flat flower. Anything bigger and the end result will not look like an ornament. Also, the yellow flowers provide a golden hue. With the foam ball safely hooked on the banana stand, you can begin inserting the pom-poms in the foam until the whole "ornament" is covered. Leave room for a few red pom-poms, which act like ruby jewels accenting the ornament.

6 Battery-operated miniature lights are available at your local crafts store. They're great for centerpieces year-round because you don't need to plug them in. And they're perfect for this arrangement. Wrap the pine branch with the lights, flick on the switch, and you've got a stand-alone branch and ornament. Let the holidays begin!

ANOTHER METHOD

Instead of using fishing line to hold the floral foam, you can wrap it in chicken wire, as in the manzanita topiary arrangement on page 97, then connect the chicken wire to the hook with fishing line or another piece of wire.

Floral Menorah

LEVEL OF EASE: 4
ETW (ESTIMATED TIME OF WOW): 1½ hours
RECOMMENDED SNACK: Almond cookies

WHAT YOU'LL NEED

9 calla lilies
9 floral stem wires
1 long container
1 plastic liner
1 brick of floral foam
Bag of blue marbles

I like to celebrate Hanukkah because the lighting of the menorah is such a beautiful tradition. Besides, the official meal of Hanukkah is dinner at a Chinese restaurant, so what's not to love? This floral menorah is truly elegant, and the calla lilies look like candles with an ever-burning flame.

1 Support the calla lily stems with floral wire. One lily at a time, poke the wire into the head of the flower and wrap it around the stem. This keeps the flower upright.

2 Line a long container with plastic, and place wet floral foam within the liner. Insert the nine calla lilies into the foam, making the middle one taller than the four on either side. Then cover the foam with the blue marbles.

Silk Stockings

LEVEL OF EASE: 1
ETW (ESTIMATED TIME OF WOW): 5 minutes
RECOMMENDED SNACK: Milk and cookies

WHAT YOU'LL NEED

Assorted artificial flowers—for example, poinsettias, pine, and holiday fruits
Stocking

I used to keep my stockings empty until Santa arrived, but filling them with silk flowers in the meantime certainly makes the holidays cheerier.

1 Place artificial stems in the stocking so that the flowers and foliage rest on the rim of the stocking. Vary the stems so you have a mix of flowers, artificial fruit, and berries.

2 When you replace the flowers with actual gifts, set the flowers in a bowl or basket by the hearth.

Holiday Ice Sculpture

'Tis the season to make these stunning ice sculptures, with artificial flowers and greenery frozen in ice.

LEVEL OF EASE: 2
ETW (ESTIMATED TIME OF WOW): 15 minutes, with overnight freezing
RECOMMENDED SNACK: Hot fudge sundae

Helpful Hint

Test the colorfastness of the silk roses before putting them in the mold. Some artificial flowers are dyed with color that runs in water, and you want to avoid those.

1 Place the silk roses, pine, and other items in the silicone bundt pan, interlacing the bead garland throughout the flowers. Nothing should be above the rim line of the bundt pan.

2 Pour water into the pan until it's about three-quarters full. Don't worry if the flowers and foliage float a little on the water.

3 Place the pan on a plate, and store in the freezer overnight.

4 After the water is completely frozen, the items that have floated above the water line are frozen in that position. Add cold water to the rest of the pan, and place the whole mold in the freezer again. Now everything will be frozen under water.

5 When the entire contents are frozen, peel off the bundt cake mold and unveil your ice sculpture. Present it on a platter surrounded by decorative foliage, like magnolia leaves. I also added some pine to the middle of the bundt sculpture, just like they did in *My Big Fat Greek Wedding*.

Part Two
Flowers in Home Décor

As you've seen from the projects presented so far in this book, flowers don't need to be relegated to vases, and this section on home décor takes this notion a step further. From taper candles sitting atop clouds of hydrangeas to a bathtub surrounded by colorful blooms, these innovative arrangements will inspire you to find room for flowers in every room of the house.

Chapter 11

In the Bedroom

The next time you watch television or go to the movies, notice a curious phenomenon. Whether a character is juggling the responsibilities of having sixteen children, trying to subvert an international espionage ring, or saving the planet from an oncoming asteroid, if a scene is shot in the bedroom there are flowers on the nightstand. Why is that? It's simple. Flowers add an air of tranquillity and romance to any room, even if it's the bedroom of a cyborg alien.

Rose Topiary

LEVEL OF EASE: ④
ETW (ESTIMATED TIME OF WOW): 1 hour
RECOMMENDED SNACK: Scones

WHAT YOU'LL NEED

50 (approx.) spray roses, in two different colors
1 candle holder with 3-inch spiked tray
Floral tape
½ brick of floral foam

Topiaries are so blueblood *Room with a View*, but the way I make them, even we commoners can enjoy these elegant arrangements.

1 Carve the floral foam into some semblance of a globe shape. It's similar to the foam ball for the ornament on page 86, but it will be bigger. I have never carved a perfect sphere. It is always lopsided, or looks like it's been sat on. Do the best you can, and it will be close enough.

2 After soaking the foam ball in water, place it on the candle holder so that the spike in the tray goes through the bottom of the foam. Attach the foam more securely with florist tape so that it doesn't wiggle on the candle holder when you move it around.

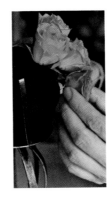

3 Spray roses, which are small, work well for this project because they are easier to line up on the foam to create a more pleasing round shape. Begin at the top and insert each rose so that the flowers are on the same level. I've chosen two separate colors of spray roses. As you go down, vary the colors at random points. If your floral foam is a little lopsided, don't worry. In the places where the foam is flatter, leave longer stems on the roses so that they jut out farther, and in the places where the foam is higher, insert the stems farther to make up for the extra height of the foam.

Broadway's *Bloopers*

One of the problems with this topiary is that the roses are a little too pointy and not open enough. When they're not open, they don't line up flush against each other. Also, the stems are uneven. Still, there is a free-form quality to this arrangement that's kind of fun. Another example of a "mistake" that Broadway should be proud of.

Magnolia Blanket Throw

LEVEL OF EASE: 1
ETW (ESTIMATED TIME OF WOW): 30 minutes
RECOMMENDED SNACK: A slice of pizza

WHAT YOU'LL NEED

10 (approx.) silk magnolias
Chenille blanket throw with fringes

Dress up a chenille throw with silk flowers for instant beauty. It's also a great way to customize a gift for a friend.

1 I've used silk magnolias for this project because of their flat profile. You don't want something jutting out at you from the blanket. Cut the magnolias so that no piece of the stem is sticking out.

2 Starting at the edge of the throw, loop the fringe around the bottom petals of the flower and tie a single knot.

3 Evenly space out the flowers by keeping track of the number of fringes between each flower. There should be room for about ten flowers. I don't recommend putting flowers on both sides of the throw, even though there is fringe on both sides, because too many flowers are overkill and can take away from the comfort of the throw.

Quiet Sign

LEVEL OF EASE: 4
ETW (ESTIMATED TIME OF WOW): 40 minutes, not including the cardboard sign
RECOMMENDED SNACK: Chocolate-dipped strawberries

WHAT YOU'LL NEED

16 (approx.) spray roses
Dental floss
Lei needle
Cardboard sign
2 paper clips
Tape

With a beautiful handle made of spray roses, this sign could say, "Shut your trap and get lost," and you still wouldn't offend anyone.

USING A LEI NEEDLE

Lei needles come in various lengths (I used a 12-inch needle), and the best part about them is that instead of an eye to feed a thread through, they have a hook. They sell them everywhere in Hawaii, but you can buy them on the Internet. I've listed some resources at the back of the book. You can also use a long sewing needle, but it's not going to be as much fun.

1 Cut a 24-inch length of dental floss and thread it through the lei needle so you have a double thickness of floss that's 12 inches long. I use dental floss when I work with lei needles because it's much easier to work with than regular thread, and it's extremely sturdy. I don't recommend fishing line because it's too stiff to use with the needles, and it's nearly impossible to create a double strand with the inflexible filament.

2 For half the spray roses, insert the lei needle through the center of the petals and out the stem. Pull the roses down on the floss after they've been threaded.

3 For the remaining half of the roses, insert the lei needle through the base of the flower first, so that it comes out the center of the petals. Pull them down on the floss. Now you should have half the roses facing one way, and half facing another. This way, when the handle hangs on a doorknob, all the roses will face downward.

4 Tie the two ends of the rose handle to paper clips, and cut off any excess floss.

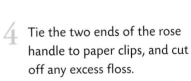

5 Tape the paper clips along the back of a Do Not Disturb sign. I made my sign on the computer and mounted it to a piece of cardboard. The roses on the handle will dry nicely, so this sign will last a while.

🐾 *Florist Secret:* How to Make a Manzanita Topiary

WITH KELLIE TUMM OF KLT FLORAL IN SANTA MONICA, CALIFORNIA

Okay, this is the type of arrangement where I throw my hands up and say, "Why bother? How can I ever do anything this beautiful?" But floral designer Kellie Tumm, who has been featured on several television wedding shows, and whose boutique studio caters to an exclusive roster of who's who in the arts and entertainment, showed me that it's a lot easier than it looks.

1 Manzanita trees can be found at many crafts stores, bird supply stores, and online. A manzanita tree that you buy is not the actual tree, but just a branch from it, without leaves or flowers. They're usually attached to square wooden bases. Place the base of the tree in a square container, and weigh it down with rocks. If you'd like, you can also fill the container with floral foam and add flowers for a more elaborate arrangement.

2 Carve floral foam into small pieces. They don't have to be round. Even with a square piece of foam, you will get a rounded shape when you insert flowers at an angle.

5 Insert flowers into the foam at an angle to create a rounded shape. The chicken wire gives the stems additional support so the flowers stay put, even when upside down.

6 You can also hang votives and beads on the branches for a very dramatic effect.

3 Wrap the foam in chicken wire. Use the open ends of the wire to hook onto the looped ends, so the foam stays secured.

4 Wedge the chicken-wired foam between two branches, and wrap wire around it to keep it in place.

Chapter 12

Sacred Spaces

As an interior designer, I meet many people trying to carve out private spaces in their home where they can meditate, read, listen to music, or just eat chocolate. Few people have an extra room they can devote entirely to this pursuit, so many folks have to convert the corner of a room, a window alcove, even the end of a hallway. Of course, flowers are absolutely crucial to these areas because they represent nature in its purest form. And what a lovely thing to meditate upon.

Bollywood Curtain

LEVEL OF EASE: ⑤
ETW (ESTIMATED TIME OF WOW): 4 hours
RECOMMENDED SNACK: Yogurt

WHAT YOU'LL NEED

12 (approx.) marigolds per strand
12 (approx.) colored straws per strand
16 feet of waxed dental floss per strand
A lei needle
1 3M Command Strip cable holder per strand

First, you'll need a room divider for your meditation area. While wooden screens or curtains will perform this function, here's a divider that's simply transcendental. I was inspired by the Bollywood movies of India, in which every scene is dripping with glorious flowers. Step behind this curtain and you've entered another realm.

1 Hook a 16-foot length of dental floss onto the needle so that you have a double strand of floss that's 8 feet long—the height of a standard ceiling. Tie a knot at the bottom of the floss to keep the marigolds from slipping past the end. It's a good idea to wrap some clear or masking tape around the knot to make this barrier even larger. Take a 1-inch piece of tape, place the knot in the middle of it, and fold the ends of the tape together.

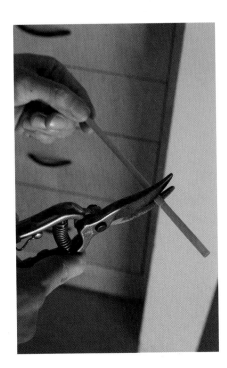

2 Cut the marigolds so almost none of the stem is left. You want little "balls" of marigolds. Then cut the drinking straws to 6-inch lengths. The straws will act as spacers for the marigolds so that each is an equal distance away from the other.

3   Insert the needle at the base of the first marigold, through the stem, and out through the top of the flower. Pull it down to the end of the dental floss, where the tape barrier is. The tape is hidden at the bottom of the string of marigolds, so it's hardly noticeable.

4   After each marigold, string a straw so you alternate flowers and straws, until you have a complete strand.

5   Tie a knot at the top of the floss to create a loop. On the ceiling, apply a 3M Command Strip, and hang the loop on the hook. (The strips come off without damaging the paint.) If you have "cottage cheese" ceilings, you'll have to install hooks with screws where there is a stud. Stringing the marigolds was a lot of work, but now you can relax and find your inner peace.

Floating Candles

LEVEL OF EASE: 1
ETW (ESTIMATED TIME OF WOW): 2 minutes
RECOMMENDED SNACK: S'mores

Tea lights sit on floating flowers in this calming display.

1   Fill a large bowl with water.

2   Float two dahlias in the water. I love dahlias because they come in vivid colors, and when a dahlia opens it has a shape similar to a water lily.

3   Set a tea light in the center of each open dahlia.

WHAT YOU'LL NEED

2 dahlias
2 tea lights
Large bowl

Lavender Zen Garden

WHAT YOU'LL NEED

1 cup of lavender potpourri
1 shallow plate or candle tray
4 or 5 rocks
A fork

Zen gardens are usually made with sand. This one is filled with lavender potpourri to add aromatherapy to your relaxation.

1 Pour lavender into the plate.

2 Spread it evenly with the fork.

3 Scatter the rocks where your heart tells you to.

4 With most zen gardens, you use a small rake to create lines in the sand. This zen garden, however, takes you to a peaceful place when you take the fork and compact the lavender in the plate. There's comfort in the order you are creating.

 Florist Secret: A Different Twist on Floral Foam

FEATURING DAVID HAHN OF WILLEM-AIDAN IN SANTA MONICA AND SAN DIEGO, CALIFORNIA

In some arrangements the flowers sit in a vase of water, while in others they're supported in floral foam. But David Hahn showed me a technique that's the best of both worlds. David's company, Willem-Aidan, is a unique luxury brand, and has been the official florist to the Cannes Film Festival, the SAG Awards, and my favorite, the *American Idol* finals.

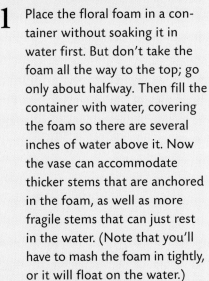

1 Place the floral foam in a container without soaking it in water first. But don't take the foam all the way to the top; go only about halfway. Then fill the container with water, covering the foam so there are several inches of water above it. Now the vase can accommodate thicker stems that are anchored in the foam, as well as more fragile stems that can just rest in the water. (Note that you'll have to mash the foam in tightly, or it will float on the water.)

2 David starts with a sculptural concept, in this case an ascending staircase, created with roses with gradually longer stems, placed in the floral foam.

3 He then adds flowers around this central structure, with some in the foam and others in the water. There's plenty of flexibility.

4 As he was creating this arrangement, David shared another tip: If you don't like it, change it. The floral foam is very forgiving, especially since you don't see it under the water. So when he was done, I asked him to take the arrangement apart and make another one using the same flowers. The glorious "rearrangement" shows that you don't have to be afraid to experiment, because you can always start over.

Chapter 13

Bath Time

Long ago, in the prehistoric days before home improvement warehouses, bathrooms were plain, utilitarian closets. Now they're the most remodeled rooms in the house, with every luxurious amenity imaginable. So here are some ideas to create your own oasis in the bathroom, even if you don't have the budget for Jacuzzi jets, a steam sauna, or Carrera marble. "Jonathan, take me away!"

Bathtub Paradise

LEVEL OF EASE: ⑤
ETW (ESTIMATED TIME OF WOW): 3 hours
RECOMMENDED SNACK: Bonbons

WHAT YOU'LL NEED

3 dozen (approx.) roses
2 dozen (approx.) Gerber daisies
3 bunches of solidasters
3 bunches of horsetail
3 bunches of snapdragons
3 dozen (approx.) medium-size leaves, like
    geranium or ivy
Various foliage and greenery
10 (approx.) disposable aluminum mini loaf tins
3 (approx.) 9 x 9 disposable brownie tins
6 (approx.) disposable potpie tins
10 (approx.) bricks of floral foam
Note: These flowers are just suggestions. You can vary
    them depending on occasion or mood, like an all-red
    color scheme for Valentine's Day or all tropical
    flowers to feel like you're really getting away.

This is quite possibly the most decadent and indulgent floral project in the book—a lush garden of flowers and shrubs surrounding a bathtub and enveloping you in floral splendor. Yet it's surprisingly easy to construct, lasts a long time, and is easy to take apart. And you know what? You deserve it.

1 Line the rim of the bathtub with the aluminum tins. They keep the floral foam and flowers in place so nothing clogs your drain. And in a week or so when the flowers have exhaled their last breath, the self-contained units make disposal a breeze. The mini loaf tins are perfect for most of the tub rim because they are so narrow. In the corners of the tub area where there is more room, you can place the larger brownie tins. And if you have special areas, like faucets, that you want to cover with flowers, the little potpie tins will fit very nicely. There are no set rules for which tins go where. Experiment with your own bathtub.

Helpful Hint

You'll probably want to avoid placing tins at the entrance of the tub. You don't want to have to crawl over flowers to get in.

2 Cut the floral foam into pieces that will fit in the various tins. Soak the pieces in water and place them in the tins.

3 You don't want aluminum staring at you when you're soaking in the tub, so you have to cover it up. Insert the leaves you've chosen—in the photographs I used geranium leaves—into the foam so that each leaf hangs down and covers the aluminum. Continue until all the aluminum in front is covered.

MAKING IT LAST

This bathtub arrangement will last a good week. As flowers wilt, you can replenish them with fresh ones to extend the life of the project. The foliage that has a longer life-span can remain as you add new flowers. This bathtub project actually lasted almost three weeks as the home-owner kept replacing the old flowers with new ones.

4 Next, add flowers and foliage to fill up the tins. There's an easy way to arrange the flowers so it doesn't look like a random mess. Group them so you have a clump of roses, a clump of daisies, a clump of solidasters, etc. That's how flowers grow in a garden—in groups. Also, insert the flowers so that the ones in front are lower than the ones in back, so you see all the blooms. Finally, in the corners, add height with taller flowers like snapdragons and horsetail.

The Fairest Mirror of Them All

Your reflection will look lovelier than ever when fresh flowers frame your bathroom mirror.

LEVEL OF EASE: ②

ETW (ESTIMATED TIME OF WOW): 45 minutes

RECOMMENDED SNACK: An apple

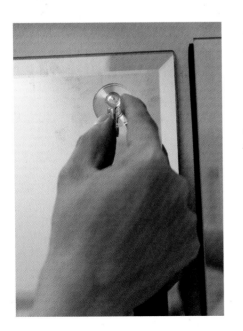

1 Apply suction cups in the four corners of the mirror, plus at the midpoint of the top and bottom.

2 Loop fishing line around the hooks, going to each suction cup until the line is strung around the perimeter of the mirror. I use fishing line here because it's almost invisible, but strong enough to hold flowers.

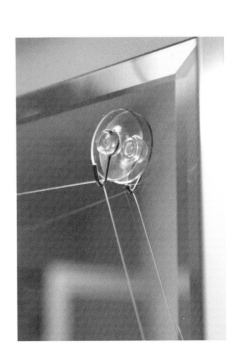

Helpful Hint

If you'd like this arrangement year-round, you can substitute silk ivy and flowers. It will still look quite heavenly.

3 Wrap strands of ivy around the fishing line until ivy completely frames the mirror.

4 Tuck flowers between the ivy and the mirror. Wrap flowers with longer stems around the ivy.

Toilet Paper Vase

LEVEL OF EASE: 1
ETW (ESTIMATED TIME OF WOW): 5 minutes
RECOMMENDED SNACK: Pepperidge Farm Mint Milanos

1 Tie a ribbon around the bathroom tissue roll.

2 Place three orchids in the hole of the bathroom tissue roll. Dendrobium orchids are usually sold with the water tubes attached. Be sure to refill the water in the tube to keep the orchids alive. If your orchids didn't come with water tubes, you can buy them at a floral supply store. Better yet, whenever you get roses from a florist, save the tubes that come with them for uses like this.

WHAT YOU'LL NEED

3 dendrobium orchids in
   water tubes
Bathroom tissue roll
Ribbon

Artfully (and discreetly) display your extra bathroom tissue rolls by turning them into flower vases.

❧ Florist Secret

Most people use tap water for their vase arrangements, but hard water, which is high in alkalines, actually reduces the life of cut flowers. That's why when you buy a bunch of orchids, or many other flowers, from the florist or market, they come with a packet of floral preservative. This "floral food" contains enough acid to neutralize the alkalines. Of course, using distilled water also solves the problem. And remember that orchids are generally tropical flowers from warm climates, so the water should not be below 50 degrees.

Chapter 14

Home Office Romance

Most people who work from home have the Puritan logic that their home office must be the one room in the house that is all business, without a trace of fun or personality. I guess they didn't get the memo. When I design home offices for clients, I emphasize that the room requires more than just organization and functionality. It also should have an element of creativity to spark productivity. A sterile environment does not feed the mind. But one filled with ideas inspires great things. Why do I suddenly sound like a fortune cookie?

Rose Trash Can

WHAT YOU'LL NEED

40 (approx.) silk roses
Wire mesh trash can
Fishing line

I believe that adding beauty to the most basic of items is what creativity is all about. And you can't get much more utilitarian than a trash can. With silk roses attached to the rim, it's also a beautiful umbrella stand or a pleasing organizer for rolls of wrapping paper.

LEVEL OF EASE: 3
ETW (ESTIMATED TIME OF WOW): 1½ hours
RECOMMENDED SNACK: Peanut butter and jelly sandwich

1 Rather than buying individual stems of silk roses, buy them in bunches, eight to nine roses per bunch. My local dollar store sells these rose bunches year-round for 99 cents. Then cut the silk roses off their stems. I've chosen two different colors of roses, but you can also limit them to one color.

2 Cut a piece of fishing line that is about 10 inches long, and tie a loop around the back of each rose, under the bottom petals.

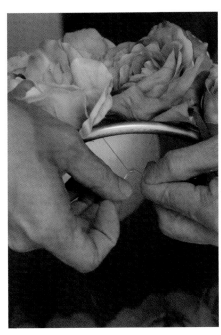

3 Starting at the top of the trash can, take the two ends of the fishing line and stick it through two holes in the mesh, about an inch apart. Pull the rose tight against the wire mesh and tie a double knot to secure the rose to the can. Snip the excess fishing line with scissors. Then repeat, placing roses adjacent to each other until you finish one row. Two rows of flowers are enough for this project. Covering the entire trash can would make it look like a big floral lampshade. Creativity in the office is one thing. Being too frou frou is another.

Orchid Bookend

LEVEL OF EASE: 2
ETW (ESTIMATED TIME OF WOW): 20 minutes
RECOMMENDED SNACK: Fish sticks

WHAT YOU'LL NEED

1 artificial orchid
2 artificial leaves
1 skinny, rectangular clear vase
Decorative rocks

This bookend has a beautiful simplicity, and it's made with just a glass vase and artificial flowers.

1 Line the bottom of the vase with rocks.

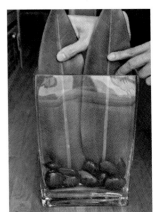

2 Insert two artificial leaves along the back of the vase, securing the stems in the rocks.

3 Tuck an artificial orchid within the vase. You will probably have to bend the orchid to fit the entire flower.

4 Cut the leaves so that they are even with the rim of the vase.

ANOTHER IDEA

The same concept, but using fresh orchids and leaves in water, makes a stunning minimalist arrangement.

Pencil Vase

LEVEL OF EASE: **2**
ETW (ESTIMATED TIME OF WOW): 20 minutes
RECOMMENDED SNACK: Chips and salsa

WHAT YOU'LL NEED

Flowers of your choice
   (I chose sweet pea and ranunculus)
35 (approx.) yellow pencils
1 tumbler
1 cloth or plastic measuring tape
1 rubber band

This is another variation of the drinking straw arrangement, this time using pencils. You'll see that there is no end to the possibilities for this type of vase arrangement. Any long, thin objects can be wrapped around a tumbler for high impact. Think chopsticks, uncooked fettuccine, artists' brushes, drumsticks (the percussion kind, not the poultry), knitting needles—the list goes on.

1 Place a rubber band around the middle of a tumbler.

2 Insert yellow pencils between the rubber band and tumbler, with the erasers at the bottom.

3 Hide the rubber band with a measuring tape, and tie a bow with it.

4 Turn the pencils so the writing on each one faces out.

5 Add flowers.

☙ *Florist Secret*

To determine how many flowers you should put in a vase, use the "four times," or 4x, rule. The space occupied by the blooms, when you view them from above, should be approximately four times the size of the vase opening. This will result in an arrangement that's full and well-proportioned.

Chapter 15

Dining in Style

If you could invite five famous people to dinner, who would they be? On the top of my list would be Olivia Newton-John, since I'm her most hopelessly devoted fan. Next, I would invite Oprah Winfrey, because not only would she be a great conversation-alist, she would probably bring a great host gift—like a car. I'd love to have Broadway diva Patti LuPone so we could sing a duet from *Evita*. Rachael Ray, so she can help me in the kitchen. And comedienne Margaret Cho, who's so funny and is also a big Olivia fan. You can bet if they were all over, my table would be set to the nines with these floral projects.

Salad Bouquet

LEVEL OF EASE: ②

ETW (ESTIMATED TIME OF WOW): 10 minutes

RECOMMENDED SNACK: Bread sticks

WHAT YOU'LL NEED

1 bell pepper: yellow, red, or orange

Spinach leaves

2 asparagus spears, blanched

2 baby carrots

Italian parsley

2 endive leaves

1 cherry tomato

Balsamic vinegar

Olive oil

In the world of fine dining, presentation is everything, and this "arrangement" turns a simple salad into a work of art.

1 A bell pepper will act as the salad's vase. I recommend a pepper that's a color other than green because there will already be enough green in the main part of the salad. Also, select a bell pepper that has a square bottom so it sits on its own. Cut off the top of the pepper and discard the seeds and membranes. Set the pepper on a plate.

2 Start by placing washed spinach leaves in the bell pepper, fanning them out so they create a dome shape in the pepper. Then add asparagus, baby carrots, parsley, and endive to the "arrangement," balancing the colors, textures, and shapes. For the salad's final splash of color, add a cherry tomato. Then drizzle olive oil and balsamic vinegar on the plate next to the bell pepper. Bon appétit!

Helpful Hint

Sometimes it's hard to find a bell pepper that will sit straight up. In that case, cut a piece off the bottom to create a flat edge.

Floral Votives

LEVEL OF EASE: ③

ETW (ESTIMATED TIME OF WOW): 15 minutes per votive

RECOMMENDED SNACK: Blueberry muffin

WHAT YOU'LL NEED

Pom-poms of various colors
Eucalyptus berries
1 "old fashioned" glass
1 small glass votive holder
1 votive candle or tea light
1 skewer
Glass marbles

Flowers nestled between an ordinary drinking glass and a glass votive holder will filter the candlelight to magnificent effect in these unique luminaries.

1 Place glass marbles at the bottom of the glass so that when you put the votive in the glass, the rim of the glass and the rim of the votive are even with each other.

2 Tuck pom-poms between the drinking glass and the votive. Use a skewer to push them down, since your fingers won't fit. On top of the pom-poms, squeeze in the eucalyptus berries, or even another row of pom-poms of a different color.

3 Place a candle in the votive holder and let the light dance around the table.

Broadway's Bloopers

When I first started making these votives, I constantly had a problem with scrunched flower petals. The flowers were flat, so they fit between the glasses, but the petals kept folding back. Even with a skewer, it was difficult to straighten out the petals. Now I avoid flowers with long petals altogether. That's why I use small pom-poms. However, here's another idea. Remove the petals and place *them* between the glasses, instead of the entire flower. They'll look like colorful feathers stacked on top of each other, with candlelight pouring through the petals.

Lavender Napkin Rings

WHAT YOU'LL NEED

Bunches of dried lavender
Raffia ribbon
Pieces of cardboard with
  guests' names on them

These simple napkin rings serve as place cards as well as party favors for your guests to take home.

1 Tie about five stems of dried lavender together with raffia.

2 Place one end of the raffia through a hole in the corner of the name card.

3 Wrap the raffia around a rolled napkin and tie a bow.

LEVEL OF EASE: ①
ETW (ESTIMATED TIME OF WOW): 3 minutes per ring
RECOMMENDED SNACK: Cheese and crackers (I like Brie)

Florist Secret: How to Make a Multi-level Pave Arrangement

FEATURING THE FLORAL DESIGNERS AT EFFUSIVE FLOWERS IN LOS ANGELES, CALIFORNIA

From the moment I stepped into Effusive Flowers, they took me under their wing and showered me with helpful tips. When I told them I had done a lot of pave-type box arrangements (straight, flat planes of densely packed flowers), they taught me how to take the idea a step further by going multi-level. I was inspired.

1 Start with a box container. If it's not water-tight, seal the seams with hot glue, as they do at Effusive, or line the box with a plastic liner. Then soak floral foam in water and place it in the container.

2 As with flat pave arrangements, mentally divide the box into sections. In the first section, place three rows of three roses. Cut the stems to the same length so the roses are at the same level. This is the highest plane of the arrangement. Now let's step down to the next level.

3 Surround the roses with bells of Ireland, also cutting the stems so they are the same length. They should be just high enough to cover the naked rose stems. Going a level lower, add a quadrant of freesias, again all at the same height. Because freesias have a natural bend to them, insert them so they fall into the arrangement, rather than out. Before moving on, cover any exposed foam with sheet moss, using greening pins.

4 The part I got really excited about was putting a row of green apples on the bottom. Drive a floral pick into the bottom of four apples, and then insert the pick into the foam. Floral picks—wooden stakes with one pointed end—can be found at most crafts stores.

5 For the final level, cut little pieces of bells of Ireland and create a frame around the entire box. Finally, tie a bow around the vertical stems.

Chapter 16

Living Room Entertaining

By incorporating flowers into home décor, you can bring function to the flowers, and that makes them even more beautiful. See how they transform these ordinary accessories in a living room into living art, giving you an indoor garden party any time of year.

Hydrangea Candlesticks

I love the Old World atmosphere these candlesticks create. I feel like there should be someone playing the harp as we look out over the pastures.

1 Take the one-third brick of floral foam and carve a cylinder that's about 3 inches in diameter and 2 inches high. Then soak the foam in water. Push a taper candle through the center of the foam. The foam will give way for the candle, and the displaced water will run off, so get ready to soak up the excess with a towel or sponge.

LEVEL OF EASE: ④

ETW (ESTIMATED TIME OF WOW): 1 hour, 15 minutes per candlestick

RECOMMENDED SNACK: Fruit salad

2 Lift the foam, and continue to push the candle all the way through. Place the candle in the candlestick and let the foam rest on top of the candlestick. Try choosing a candlestick with a lip on it. Otherwise, gravity might make the foam drop and not stay in position.

3 Each hydrangea stem is a big bush, so snip the individual blossoms and insert them around the foam. Don't completely cover the foam, though, because you'll add some roses later. The foam is only 3 inches wide, but the hydrangeas greatly increase the circumference of the floral arrangement to provide a nice, rounded shape.

4 Spray roses will add some extra color and texture, complementing the hydrangeas beautifully. Insert them in groups of two or three around the hydrangeas.

5 Accent the arrangement with little sprigs of berries. Last, wrap the flowers with ivy, anchoring it to the foam with greening pins.

Helpful Hint

Make sure that the candle fits into the candlestick first. You'd think there would be standard sizes, but I rarely find perfect fits. Therefore, it's good to know ahead of time if you need to shave the candle base a little bit, or add a bit of wax on the side to broaden it. Once the foam is around the candle, it's harder to make adjustments.

Tray Chic

LEVEL OF EASE: ②
ETW (ESTIMATED TIME OF WOW): 45 minutes
RECOMMENDED SNACK: Orange slices

WHAT YOU'LL NEED

Moss
12 roses
Rose petals
2 serving trays, one smaller than the other

This serving tray is a traveling garden.
Now, how refreshing is that?

1 Sit the smaller tray in the larger tray. Squeeze moss between the two trays to hold them in place. Leave the corners empty.

2 Place three roses in each corner. You don't need water or floral foam. Just place the buds between the two trays, and they'll dry like that.

3 Sprinkle rose petals in the smaller tray.

✤ *Florist Secret:* How to Make a Modular Pave Arrangement

FEATURING CATHERINE KIM OF CATHERINE KIM FLORAL DESIGN IN
VENICE, CALIFORNIA

I love Catherine's work because she's so inventive. A beautifully made arrangement isn't enough for her. Here, she groups four pave arrangements as a centerpiece that can also be modular, so individual pieces can be scattered around the living room. As an added bonus, each also holds a tea light candle.

The Coasters

LEVEL OF EASE: ②
ETW (ESTIMATED TIME OF WOW): 15 minutes
RECOMMENDED SNACK: Chocolate chip cookies

WHAT YOU'LL NEED

Sheet moss
Miscellaneous flowers like daisies and mums
4-inch terra cotta saucer
Poster putty

Instead of setting your drinks on the table, place them on these lawn-like coasters. The base is a shallow terra cotta saucer, filled with sheet moss that absorbs any moisture.

1 Soak the moss in water and wring out any excess moisture.

2 Pack the moss into the terra cotta saucer. If it's too lumpy, put a weight on it overnight.

3 Wrap a flower with poster putty and stick it on the edge of the terra cotta saucer.

1 Use four ceramic vases that are of different heights and sizes, but of uniform color.

2 Place wet floral foam in each vase up to the rim.

3 Using the Straight-in Method (see page 13), insert a different type and color of flower in each vase.

4 Leave a hole in the middle where you'll place a tea light candle.

5 Group them together one day, separate them the next, place them in pairs the day after, and so on. The combinations are endless.

Part Three

Flowers in Fashion

Florals have been a fashion staple ever since Adam and Eve debuted their matching fig leaf ensembles for the Winter 00 Collection. It makes perfect sense. Whether they're fresh or artificial, flowers can add drama to your wardrobe from head to toe. And they can add new life to an old piece of clothing, making it a one-of-a-kind fashion statement. Fashion trends may come and go, but flowers are here to stay.

Chapter 17

Runway Fabulous

I love flowers in the home so much that I wanted to incorporate them in clothing and accessories as well. Not being particularly adept with a sewing machine, I consulted some fashion experts to help me out. And I learned I didn't necessarily even need a sewing machine.

Fleur Couture

I first saw fashion designer Stacey Barker's work at a fashion show for the California Design College/Art Institute. She bowled me over with her witty creations, particularly her showstopping gown, which was completely festooned with multi-colored silk flowers. I was even more stunned when she showed me how easy it was to attach the flowers to the dress.

LEVEL OF EASE: ②
ETW (ESTIMATED TIME OF WOW): 1 minute per flower
RECOMMENDED SNACK: Water with lemon

1 Glue a flat-backed safety pin to the silk flower.

2 Pin the flower onto the dress.

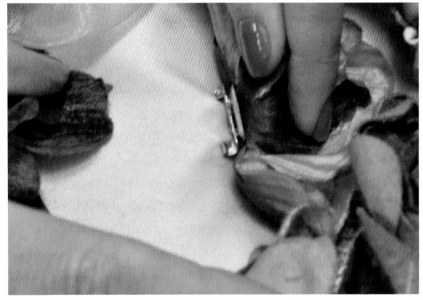

OTHER IDEAS

I realize that most people don't need such an elaborate gown. But this technique can be used with almost any article of clothing. Once you pin one silk flower, you'll want to experiment with everything in your closet. Try pinning flowers to the sleeves of a blouse, or along the hem of a pair of jeans. Finally, you'll get recognition for the fashionista you really are.

On Your Feet

Silk flowers
Silk leaves
Feathers
Hot glue gun
Small piece of leather
Shoe clip

If the shoes make the outfit, the flowers make the shoes. Popular lifestyle expert and crafter Sonya Nimri helped me design these floral shoe clips, which attach to any pair of shoes. I haven't tried them on sneakers, but you go right ahead.

LEVEL OF EASE: ③

ETW (ESTIMATED TIME OF WOW): 30 minutes

RECOMMENDED SNACK: Root beer float

1 Glue silk flowers onto the silk leaves.

2 Tuck feathers between the flowers and leaves.

3 On the back of the leaves, glue a shoe clip.

4 Cover the shoe clip by gluing on the small piece of leather, and clip the whole thing onto a shoe.

Gypsy Skirt

LEVEL OF EASE: 5
ETW (ESTIMATED TIME OF WOW): 4 hours
RECOMMENDED SNACK: Rice Krispies Treats

WHAT YOU'LL NEED

Pieces of fabric about 12 inches x 12 inches
Pins
Sewing machine
Safety pins

While ready-made silk flowers can look very dramatic, flowers sewn from satin and other fabrics have a more casual look, as you can see from this gypsy skirt. So here's an extra-credit project for those of you with some basic sewing knowledge.

1 Fold a square piece of fabric diagonally.

2 Cut the fabric 2 to 3 inches above the diagonal line.

3 Pin the two sides of the fabric piece together.

4 Now trim each end of the long piece of pinned fabric so there is a slight curve to each end. That way, when you roll the fabric into a rose (in step 7, on the next page), the tips of the "petals" will be rounded rather than squared.

5 Use a sewing machine to sew a single stitch along the open edge of the fabric, leaving a ¼-inch seam. If you don't have a sewing machine, you can hand-sew it, using an "up and over" or "through and through" stitch.

6 Slowly pull the thread to create a gather.

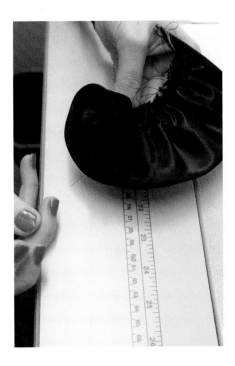

7 Roll the fabric to begin forming your rose. Pinch the bottom to create the base of the rose, and hand-sew the base, using a "through and through" stitch so the rose doesn't unravel. (The base is too thick to place in a sewing machine, so you need to hand-sew at this point.)

8 Pin the roses to your skirt with safety pins. Unlike with the silk flowers, you don't need to glue the safety pins to the sewn flowers.

Hats Off

WHAT YOU'LL NEED

6–10 fabric flowers
Safety pins
Hat

Here's another use for fabric roses (see pages 136–137). While ready-made silk flowers would make the hat look a little "grand dame," the casual look of these impromptu fabric blooms softens any formality inherent in a hat.

LEVEL OF EASE: 2 (assuming you know how to sew the flowers)

ETW (ESTIMATED TIME OF WOW): 45 minutes

RECOMMENDED SNACK: Bagel and cream cheese

1 Sew the flowers using the instructions on pages 136–137.

2 Use safety pins to attach the flowers to the hat.

Earring Blossoms

LEVEL OF EASE: 2

ETW (ESTIMATED TIME OF WOW): 2 minutes

RECOMMENDED SNACK: Corn on the cob

WHAT YOU'LL NEED

Silk hydrangeas
Stud earrings

I asked one of my friends, jewelry designer Lori Indgin, how one would assemble a pair of earrings with flowers. She said, "That's easy," and she was right.

1 Disassemble a silk hydrangea stem so that you're left with just the petals.

2 Insert the stud between the holes in the petal and attach it to the earring back.

Orchid Necklace

LEVEL OF EASE: 1
ETW (ESTIMATED TIME OF WOW): 15 minutes
RECOMMENDED SNACK: A brownie

WHAT YOU'LL NEED

2 or 3 orchid blooms
Floral stem wrap tape
½-inch organza ribbon

You may recognize Sonya Nimri from NBC's *Today Show*, where she was one of the three finalists in the Domestic Diva Contest. She also tours the country for Michael's Arts and Crafts Store and Klutz Books. Here she models a simple orchid choker that she created for us.

1 Tie the orchid stems together with stem wrap tape (see page 12).

2 Then tie the organza ribbon around the entire bunch. You can now wear it around your neck, with the orchids resting to the side. The orchids will last the entire day.

It's a Guy Thing

LEVEL OF EASE: 2
ETW (ESTIMATED TIME OF WOW): 1 hour
RECOMMENDED SNACK: Quiche

WHAT YOU'LL NEED

Silk hydrangeas
Necktie
Hot glue gun

I'm always on the lookout for cool ties. This one that Stacey Barker created for me is quite possibly the coolest. The petals of silk hydrangeas are small and flat, so they lie well on fabric. Also, because of their shape, the individual petals look like a complete flower.

1 Cut off individual blossoms from the silk hydrangea stem and remove the petals.

2 Attach the petals to the tie using the hot glue gun.

My Grandpa Oliver came to America as a young man to seek his fortune. What he found instead was hard work, isolation, and separation from a new wife and child he would not see for more than forty years. When my parents, grandmother, siblings, and I finally immigrated to this country in the '60s, Grandpa was our link to American culture. He taught me the joys of TV dinners, miniature golf, game shows, and Christmas. He is the reason I love corned-beef hash and eggs. He was the one who went to parent-teacher conferences, made cupcakes for school bake sales, and drove me to talent shows and recitals. He was always cheerful, and uncompromisingly generous. His journey here on Earth made my walk a little easier. This book is dedicated to him.

My Grandpa and my siblings, with me in the little sport coat.
Stylish even then!

Acknowledgments

Someone up there likes me. How else can I explain the dream experience that putting together this book has been? I am blessed to be surrounded by people who believe in me, support me, and nod their heads no matter how crazy my ideas might seem.

Bouquets to my team at Watson-Guptill: Joy Aquilino, Victoria Craven, Allison Devlin, and Lori Horak. And many thanks to Patricia Fogarty, Pooja Bakri, and Joseph Illidge, for being the miracle workers you are.

Laurels to my photographer, Jessica Boone. You really outdid yourself this time, my friend.

Gladiolas to everyone who allowed me to shoot in their homes and backyards: Stephanie Burns, Sandra Dupont and Miklos Fulop, Joanne Gordon, Deborah Kautzky, Erin Lareau, Dan Mayeda, Susan Rosales and Kacey Mayeda, Rena and Victor Morton, Rich Reams at Loft Appeal, and Sandi Silbert and Brian Davis. Thanks for your hospitality.

A tribute of cascading petals to the designers who contributed to this book: Elizabeth Bailey, Stacey Barker, David Hahn, Lori Indgin, Catherine Kim, Suzane LeMay, Walter Nicolas, Sonya Nimri, Roman Sacke, Kellie Tumm, and everyone at Effusive Flowers. I am inspired by your creativity and generosity.

Heaps of orchids to Cheryl Yanagida, for teaching me how to use a lei needle; my website designer, Scott Alumbaugh, who makes me look like a conglomerate already; Angie Horejsi, for coordinating and scheduling all the guest florists; and Allyson Ranallo, for proofing my manuscript and catching the incorrect title (yikes, that would've been embarrassing).

A floral cake for Kitty Bartholomew, who was the first person to have me demonstrate my floral arrangements on television. Thank you for steadying my hand when I got nervous.

A single, perfect rose for the single, most perfect agent in the world, Deborah Warren.

And finally, thanks to Greg Phillips, for the antihistamines. I've got a floral cupcake with your name on it.

Resource Directory

When I started experimenting with floral arrangements, I didn't have access to any professional sources. No fancy, trade-only places for me. Even now, I prefer shopping at my local arts and crafts store and browsing on the Internet for supplies. (It's so fun getting package deliveries in the mail!) Here is some advice on where to shop, plus a directory of the talented floral designers who've contributed to the book.

Floral Foam, Silk Flowers, and Other Floral Supplies

Floral supplies are relatively inexpensive, so pick up a few starter materials and begin experimenting. You'll find that with the right tools of the trade, you just can't go wrong. You can find them at your local crafts store and, of course, online.

Umbrellas

The colorful Monet umbrella featured in chapter 4 was from my neighborhood art supply store. There's a whole collection of these fine art umbrellas. Your local art supply store probably carries them, too.

Drinking Straws

People always ask me where I get my colorful drinking straws. I buy them at Ikea. Every season, they stock new colors, so I stock up. You can also find the straws at most party supply stores, and even supermarkets.

Rosewood Pumpkins

Exotic rosewood pumpkins like the one shown in chapter 9 make beautiful decorations throughout the fall and winter seasons.

Wood U Like
(310) 540-6393
ulikewood@yahoo.com
www.woodulike.homestead.com

Lei Needles

If you're not fortunate enough to live in Hawaii, you can buy lei needles very inexpensively on the Internet.

www.hulasource.com
www.paradiseflowers.com
www.hawaiianleis.net

Shoe Clips

You can buy these at jewelry supply stores, either in your neighborhood or online. You'll find shoe clips in the jewelry supply category called "findings."

www.bjcraftsupplies.com
www.creativefindings.com

Manzanita Trees

It's great having a manzanita tree around the house. You can decorate it for different occasions, use it to display jewelry, or just let it sit unadorned. They come in different heights to suit your needs, as well. I buy mine at a crafts store, but you can also find them at your local bird supply store (they make popular perches for parrots). Or consider shopping online.

Guest Floral Designers

Barrington Flowers
Elizabeth Bailey
11718 San Vicente Blvd.
Brentwood, CA 90049
(310) 826-2117
elizabeth@barringtonflowers.com
www.barringtonflowers.com

Catherine Kim Floral Design
Catherine Kim
(310) 351-6831
cathykim616@hotmail.com

Effusive Flowers
12204 W. Pico Blvd.
Los Angeles, CA 90064
(310) 826-4353
www.effusiveflowers.com

KLT Floral
Kellie Tumm
500 Broadway
Santa Monica, CA 90401
(310) 656-0688

Kytka Floral Design
Roman Sacke
517 ½ N. Fairfax Ave.
Los Angeles, CA 90036
(323) 951-9541
kytka@sbcglobal.net

Nicolas Flowers & Events
Walter Nicolas
P.O. Box 1142
Beverly Hills, CA 90213
(310) 289-1967
walternicolas67@aol.com

Les Sculptures Vivantes
Suzane LeMay
3763 Midvale Ave.
Los Angeles, CA 90034
(310) 202-6363
(310) 202-6386 fax

Willem-Aidan
David Hahn
www.willem-aidan.com

Fashion Designer

Stacey Barker
lalaleopard@yahoo.com

Jewelry Designers

Lori Indgin
(310) 338-1551
lori@framerz.com

Sonya Nimri
sonya@sonyastyle.com
www.sonyastyle.com

Index